THE REVIVE CAFE COOKBOOK 2

www.revive.co.nz

Copyright © Revive Concepts Limited 2012
Published by Revive Concepts Limited

ISBN 978-0-473-21751-8

Also by Jeremy Dixon: The Revive Cafe Cookbook

Produced in New Zealand
Food Photography & Styling: Jeremy Dixon
Cafe Photography: Elesha Newton
Graphic Design: Rebecca Zwitser, Jeremy Dixon & Delyce Liggett
Food Preparation: Jeremy Dixon, Maggi Foldi, Ricardo Delgado
Recipe testing and proofing: Verity Dixon, Nyree Tomkins, Dyanne Dixon, Keryn McCutcheon, Kjirstnne Jensen, Elesha Newton, Brenda Wood, Colleen Wood, Delyce Liggett, Narelle Liggett, Heather Cameron, Dawn Simpson, Megan Tooley

The publisher makes no guarantee as to the availability of the products in this book. Every effort has been made to ensure the accuracy of the information presented and any claims made; however, it is the responsibility of the reader to ensure the suitability of the product and recipe for their particular needs. Many natural ingredients vary in size and texture, and differences in raw ingredients may marginally affect the outcome of some dishes. Most recipes have been adjusted from the cafe recipes to make them more appropriate for a home kitchen. All health advice given in this book is a guideline only. Professional medical or nutritional advice should be sought for any specific issues.

Metric and imperial measurements have been used in this cookbook. The tablespoon size used is 15ml (½fl oz), teaspoon 5ml (⅙fl oz) and cup 250ml (8fl oz). Some countries use slightly different sized measurements, however these will not make a significant difference to the outcome of the recipes.

Revive Cafes
16 Fort St, Auckland Central, New Zealand
33 Lorne St, Auckland Central, New Zealand

If you like the recipes in this book we recommend you sign up for the weekly inspirational Revive e-mails.
They contain a weekly recipe, cooking and lifestyle tips, the weekly Revive menu, special offers and Revive news.
Visit www.revive.co.nz to sign up or to purchase more copies of this or our other cookbooks online.
Privacy Policy: Revive will never share your details and you can unsubscribe at any time.
LIKE us on Facebook! www.facebook.com/cafe.revive.

the revive cafe cookbook 2

Contents

Introduction

I left my corporate marketing job, took a huge risk, chased my dream, and started Revive in 2005 to provide people with healthier food. Over the past 7 years Revive has grown to 2 branches and now 2 cookbooks. It has been the adventure of my life!

In 2011 I produced the first Revive Cafe Cookbook. I was blown away by how popular it was and the emails and letters from people saying how it had transformed their lives and showed them how to cook healthier food. I comissioned a second printing within 5 months. So I thought I had better release a second book - with all the recipes that did not make it into the first, and recipes I had since developed.

I wrongly assumed that people knew how to cook healthy and just preferred unhealthy food instead. However, the responses I have been getting back indicates people really do want to be healthy, they just struggle to fit it in with their lives.

This cookbook works as a cookbook all on its own. However, combined with the first cookbook, you will have a great collection of many of Revive's favourite recipes, along with 10 step-by-step guides to customise your own creations. This book contains four sauces/dressings from the first book that are used in many of the recipes.

My mission in life is to help people have more vitality and achieve their life dreams. Too many people lack the energy to do the things that are important to them. In many cases this is due to average or poor lifestyle habits which starts with eating and drinking bad food, and missing out on key foods that give us energy and good health.

Revive food is not only vegetarian, but full of whole grains, fresh produce and natural flavour enhancing ingredients. By eating the food in this cookbook, combined with practising the 8 keys to healthy living, you will find you have more energy and vitality within a short time.

It is my desire that you achieve this health and well being in your life and are able to not only live to a good age, but have a life full of mountain top experiences along the way.

I would like to thank my lovely team at Revive who give amazing service and prepare great food. Thanks also to my dedicated team of recipe testers and proof readers who help make sure the recipes work.

I would love to hear how you find the book so please e-mail me at jeremy@revive.co.nz with your thoughts and any discoveries or ideas you may have.

Jeremy Dixon
August 2012

Cookbook Notes

Garlic, Ginger & Chilli

Garlic and ginger have amazing flavour enhancing properties and we use both extensively at Revive and in these recipes. You can just chop them up finely before adding to a dish or you can make your own purees by blending the garlic or ginger with a little oil. You can buy pureed ginger at the supermarket and this is fine.

I recommend that garlic should always be used fresh and never purchased in a puree as it has an unpleasant flavour. You can buy pre-crushed/pureed chilli in a jar which is used in some recipes (in small amounts).

Sweeteners

The recipes do not use added refined sugar. The most convenient natural sweetener is liquid honey. Alternatively make up a batch of date puree (page 157) which is an excellent and inexpensive sweetener to use.

There are also other healthy sweeteners available such as apple sauce, agave and maple syrup, but these tend to be quite expensive for everyday use.

Oils

My favourite oil is rice bran oil and is what I use wherever "oil" is used. It is one of the best oils to cook with as it can withstand higher temperatures. Also, it has a very neutral taste so is good for dressings.

Generally you should not heat olive oil.

Grape seed oil is also a good oil to use or you can use your favourite oil. In some recipes sesame oil is used and this is marked as such.

Beans/Chickpeas

I have used canned beans/chickpeas (garbanzo beans) in all of the recipes as this is the most convenient. However, if you can use freshly cooked beans they will taste better.

I recommend that you soak and cook your own beans and store them in your freezer. You will need to soak overnight in plenty of water (they expand three times their volume). Then cook in fresh water until soft, which will be between 30 minutes and 2 hours, depending on the bean and its age. Then freeze them in small containers for easy use.

To defrost, simply run some hot water over them in a sieve or colander for 30 seconds.

Nuts

Nuts are used in many dishes at Revive and in this cookbook. Roasted nuts are usually used where they are presented whole (in salads or stir fries) so they hold their crunchiness and do not go soggy. Raw nuts are generally used where they will be blended as they will give a creamier result. However, having the wrong sort of nut will not affect the outcome of most recipes as they are usually interchangeable. Where cashews or almonds are used to make a cream or milk, you can substitute sunflower seeds for a nut free version. You can use whole nuts or nut pieces if you want to minimise the costs.

Creams

Different methods are used to make some dishes creamy. Coconut cream, almond cream and cashew cream can be used interchangeably in most of the recipes.

Cooking Grains

I recommend that you cook extra grains like rice and quinoa and store in your refrigerator for an easy ingredient to use in the following few days. When you cook grains remember to use boiling water to save time, and first bring the grain to the boil before turning down to a simmer. Do not stir grains while they are cooking and keep the lid on.

Cooking Terms

Saute: to cook food on a high heat and in a little oil while stirring with a wooden spoon.
Simmer: to have food cooking at a low heat setting so it is just bubbling.
Roast: to bake in the oven covered with a little oil. Use the fan bake setting if your oven has one, this will achieve more even cooking.

Mixing

You can mix most recipes in the pot you are cooking in or in a big mixing bowl. When mixing, it is important to stir gently so as not to damage the food. With salads, mix with your hands if possible. Gently lift up the ingredients and let them fall down with gravity rather than squeezing the ingredients.

Taste Test

It is difficult to get a recipe that works 100% the same every time, especially when you are using natural and fresh ingredients. Sizes in vegetables vary, spices and herbs differ in strength and you can even get differences in evaporation rates with different sized pots.

Make sure you taste test every dish before you serve and be willing to add more seasoning or a little more cooking time if necessary.

Blenders

Some recipes require a food processor (usually with an S blade). Other recipes require a blender or liquidiser (usually a tall jug with 4 pronged blades) or stick blender.

Some hotpots require a stick blender to blend the mixture to make it smoother and more consistent, but if you don't have one don't worry as this will not alter the outcome significantly.

Quantities

The quantities for each dish are an estimate and will vary depending on cooking times and ingredient size. I have used one cup as an average serve size.

Gluten Free & Dairy Free

A large proportion of the recipes are gluten free and/ or dairy free. If you have any allergies you will need to check that each recipe is suitable and make adjustments as required.

Essentials Fridge & Freezer

Freeze and refrigerate leftovers and cooked grains/beans. Regularly stock up basic produce as required and as in season.

Freezer

berries: boysenberries, blueberries, strawberries, raspberries

cooked beans: chickpeas (garbanzo), red kidney, white, black, black-eye

corn kernels

peas

red capsicum (bell peppers) diced

spinach (usually in balls)

Refrigerator

aioli (page 156)

basil pesto (page 142)

crushed chilli

date puree (page 157)

ginger puree

hummus or other dips

leftover rice or quinoa

Revive relish (page 150)

soy sauce

sweet chilli sauce

Thai curry pastes: red, green, yellow

Produce

beetroot

broccoli

cabbage: red, white

carrots

cauliflower

celery

cucumber, telegraph

fruit: bananas, lemons, apples

garlic

herbs: mint, parsley, basil, coriander (cilantro)

kumara (sweet potato): red, orange, gold

leeks

lettuce: cos (romaine), iceberg, fancy, mesclun

mesclun lettuce

mushrooms

onions: brown, red

potatoes

pumpkin

silver beet (Swiss chard)

spring onions (scallions)

tomatoes

zucchini (courgette)

Essentials Pantry

These items are shelf stable and generally have a long life. Always keep these stocked up so you can use at any time.

Herbs & Spices

- coriander
- cumin
- curry powder
- mixed herbs
- smoked paprika
- thyme
- turmeric

General

- canned chopped tomatoes
- chickpea (besan/chana) flour
- coconut cream
- dried fruit: sultanas, raisins, prunes, dates, apricots
- honey
- oil: rice bran, olive, sesame
- olives: kalamata, black
- pasta and pasta sheets
- peanut butter, tahini (sesame seed paste)
- soy sauce or tamari
- vinegar: balsamic, cider
- whole-grain mustard

Grains

- brown rice : long grain, short grain
- bulghur wheat
- couscous: fine, Israeli
- quinoa
- rolled oats: fine, jumbo

Beans

- canned and dried beans: chickpeas (garbanzo), red kidney, white, black, black-eyed
- dried lentils: red, yellow, brown (crimson), green

Nuts & Seeds

- almonds
- brazil nuts
- cashew nuts
- poppy seeds
- sesame seeds: black, white
- shredded coconut
- sunflower seeds

The 8 Keys to Healthy Living

These are the health principles that Revive is founded on. It is not enough to just eat healthy food to have complete energy and vitality. There are other simple things that create good health, summarised by these 8 keys.

The good news is that if you apply these 8 simple steps in your day-to-day living, you will notice dramatic improvements in your vitality, health and quality of life.

1. Nutrition - eat plant-based foods, fresh produce and avoid processed foods and sugars.

2. Exercise - get 30 minutes per day.

3. Water - drink at least 2 litres (2 quarts) of pure water per day.

4. Sunshine - aim for 10 minutes minimum per day.

5. Temperance - free yourself from stimulants like alcohol, energy drinks, coffee and drugs.

6. Air - breathe deeply - start every day with 10 deep breaths.

7. Rest - get 8 hours quality sleep every night.

8. Trust - live at peace with everyone and your God.

Apart from eating healthier, the quickest way to get immediate increases in energy and vitality is by drinking water and exercise. The next 2 pages detail some easy ways to get more of these things in your life.

However, do not stop there, sign up for the regular Revive emails at www.revive.co.nz for weekly inspirational ideas and encouragement!

Water

9 easy ways to help you drink 8 glasses per day!

1. Every morning fill up your water bottles (eg. 3 x 750ml (24oz) size) with filtered water.

2. Have the bottles on your desk, in your car, in your bag. If they are at your fingertips you will find after a while you drink them automatically.

3. Feel hungry? You may well be dehydrated (the body can get confused). Link the feeling of hunger with dehydration and have a drink of water when you feel hungry and the hunger pains will most likely go away.

4. Make a list of all the health benefits you will get if you drink water (eg. happiness, smooth skin, better sleep, lose weight). Make a list of all the painful consequences if you do not drink water (eg. tiredness, wrinkles, disease, early death). Linking pleasure and pain to activities can help focus you.

5. Try a squeeze of fresh lemon in a large glass of warm water first thing in the morning. This will stimulate your liver and kidneys as well.

6. Try a hot water instead of your usual hot drink.

7. Have a friend or family member remind you and keep you accountable.

8. Ask your boss to install a water filter near to your desk or workspace.

9. If you do not like the taste - just toughen up for a week and before you know it, you will associate feeling great with water and will like drinking it.

Exercise

7 fun ways to exercise more!

1. Hire or buy a bike and go mountain biking in many of the great tracks that are around most areas. I much prefer biking on mountain trails than city streets.

2. Go for a long bush walk, there will be many nice ones in your area if you search for them.

3. Swimming is a great way to exercise with low impact.

4. Join a gym or start a boot-camp. Most will give you a complimentary membership for a week to try them out. If you struggle with commitment make sure you sign up with a personal trainer.

5. Try geocaching - where you have to search out a location on your smart-phone by satellite. Search the internet to find the locations and details. There are tens of thousands of caches around the world.

6. Skipping is an amazing way to get fit. Try to see how many minutes you can skip for. It is harder than you think. Also the boxing drill exercises (skipping, push ups, pull ups, sit ups) are awesome for your body.

7. Tennis, squash and other one-on-one games are great and also a good way to catch up with friends.

Commit to a regular time with friends and family and look forward to how great you will start to feel within a short time.

Salads

This is one of our original classic salads that is fresh, tasty and colourful! 4C stands for carrot, coriander, cashews and coconut which all blend well together!

4C Salad

MAKES 6 X 1 CUP SERVES

½ cup shredded coconut

1 cup raw cashew nuts

2 teaspoons ground coriander

2 tablespoons oil

4 carrots

¼ cup lemon dressing (page 156)

3 tablespoons honey or date puree

1 tablespoon black sesame seeds

½ cup coriander (cilantro) freshly chopped

1. In a bowl combine coconut, cashews, ground coriander and oil and mix.

2. Pour onto an oven tray and bake at 150°C (300°F) for 10 minutes or until just brown (but not burned).

3. Grate carrots.

4. Combine all ingredients in a bowl and mix gently.

Shredded Coconut

A great tasty ingredient for many salads and sweet things. It is great to use with dark coloured salads for contrast. When lightly toasted it releases some amazing flavours too. I generally get the long flakes as they have greater visual impact than the coconut "dust" varieties.

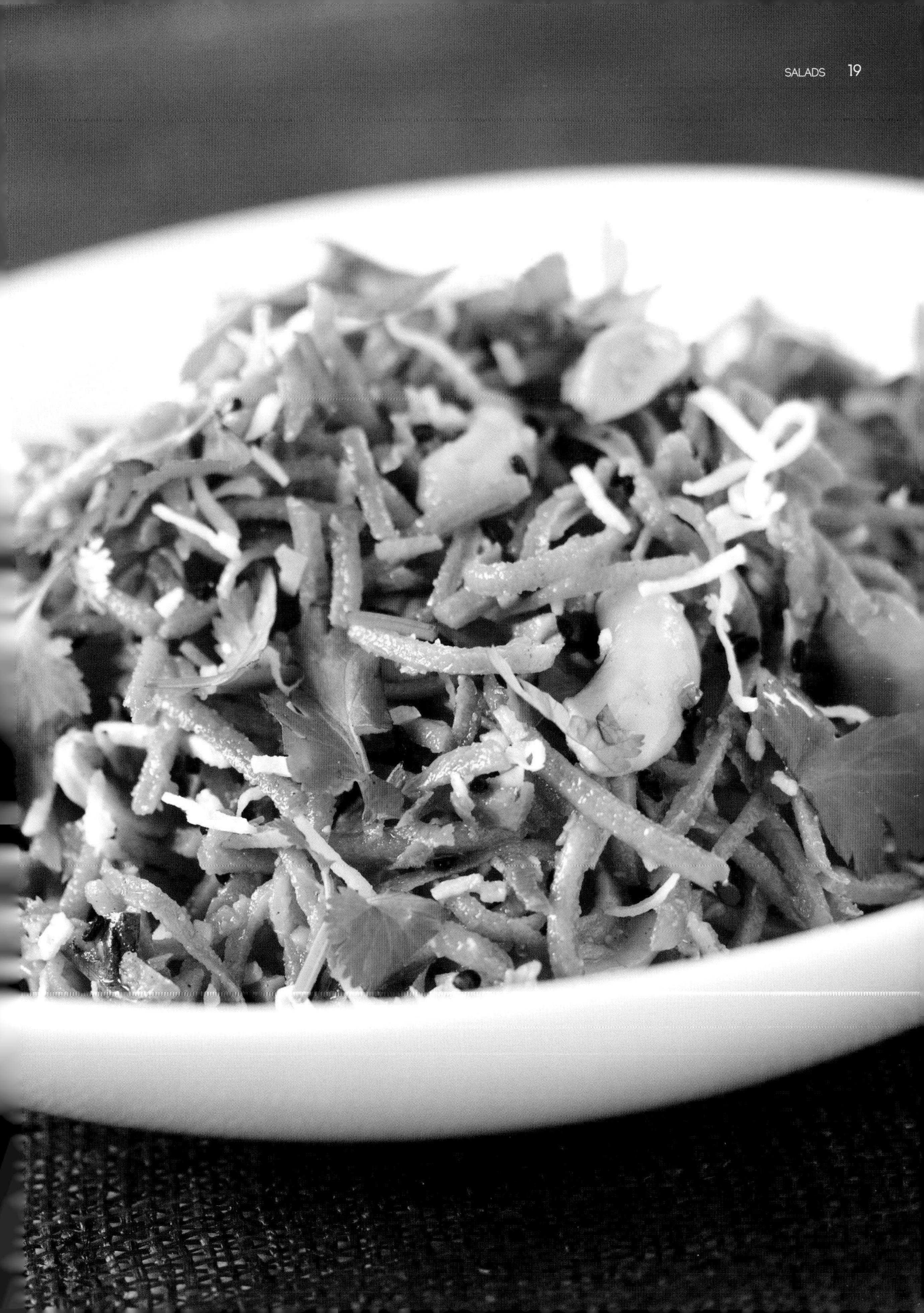

This recipe was inserted into this book at the very last minute as I discovered this easy to make salad. I needed something green so I experimented with some vegetables I found at my local Asian produce shop. I first had just the sesame oil but it lacked something so I drizzled on some liquid honey and that made the flavours explode!

Sesame Asian Greens

MAKES 10 X 1 CUP SERVES

4 pressed cups spinach

3 pressed cups bok-choy

3 pressed cups kai-lan
or choy-sum

1 red capsicum
(bell pepper)

4 tablespoons liquid honey

4 tablespoons sesame oil

½ teaspoon salt

2 tablespoons white
sesame seeds

2 tablespoons black
sesame seeds

1. Chop the green vegetables into 3cm (1½in) strips. Cut across the stalks so you break up the stringy texture.

2. Slice the capsicum into thin strips.

3. Mix vegetables in a bowl and drizzle the sesame oil and honey over the top and mix gently. Sprinkle the sesame seeds on top.

The salad greens used here are only an example combination, choose whatever varieties you have available.

While you can lightly steam these vegetables, they lose their crunch and volume significantly.

Asian Greens

There are some wonderful green Asian vegetables available at your Asian supermarket. Kai-lan, bok-choy and choy-sum are some of my favourites, although there are many more. Some are stringy so they usually need chopping through the stalk so they are easy to chew. Their white stalks are very crunchy and flavoursome so include these too.

This salad was invented for our Indian week in 2012. It is an amazing flavoursome combination of ingredients - the sweet dates and mint go well with the rice and chickpeas!

Spiced Date Pilau

MAKES 9 X 1 CUP SERVES

2 cups cooked long grain brown rice (or use ¾ cup rice and 1½ cups hot water)

400g (14oz) can chickpeas (garbanzo beans) drained

2 carrots grated

1 red onion finely diced

1 red capsicum (bell pepper) diced

½ cup diced dates

½ cup sultanas (or raisins)

½ cup roasted cashew nuts

¼ teaspoon cinnamon

¼ teaspoon clove powder

1 teaspoon ground turmeric

1 cup freshly chopped mint

1 spring onion

½ cup lemon dressing (page 156)

1. Before you start, soak the dates and sultanas in some boiling water to soften them.

2. Cook rice and water with the lid on for 25 minutes (or use pre-cooked rice).

3. Prepare all of the vegetables.

4. Drain the dates and sultanas.

5. Combine all ingredients in a bowl and mix gently.

Clove Powder

This is an amazingly fragrant ingredient to use. You can buy whole cloves however it is far easier to buy the clove powder ready to use. It is available at most Indian grocery stores.

Many 'natural' cafes have their own version of a raw or beetroot salad so I thought we had better have one at Revive too. I tried out some different versions from around the world and came up with this blend which is very delicious and easy to make!

Revive Raw Salad

MAKES 6 X 1 CUP SERVES

½ cup sultanas

2 medium beetroot

4 carrots

10 mint leaves

½ cup sunflower seeds

ORANGE DRESSING

juice of 1 orange (or ½ cup orange juice)

2 tablespoons balsamic vinegar

2 tablespoons honey or date puree

1 teaspoon salt

4 tablespoons oil

1. Put the sultanas in some boiling water before you start to fatten them and make them juicy.

2. Grate the beetroot and carrots by hand or in your food processor using the grater attachment.

3. In a cup mix the orange dressing ingredients.

4. Drain the water off the sultanas.

5. Combine all ingredients in a bowl and mix gently.

Make sure you add the juice that comes off the beetroot when you are grating it.

Mint

This delicious herb is great in sweet and savoury dishes. You can grow it easily in your garden too. Just chop it up fresh and add. It is awesome in smoothies too!

This is a great example of how flexible a lettuce salad can be with some unique and non-traditional ingredients. Cos lettuce is my favourite as it is always crisp but this will work with other lettuce varieties too.

Cos & Courgette Mingle

MAKES 9 X 1 CUP SERVES

3 zucchini (courgettes)

¼ teaspoon salt

1 tablespoon oil

1 head cos
(romaine) lettuce

1 cup diced feta cheese

1 red capsicum (bell
pepper) finely diced

optional: ¼ cup aioli
(page 156)

½ cup chopped
roasted peanuts

1. Cut zucchini long ways and then cut into half moons diagonally.

2. In a pan saute zucchini, salt and oil for about 3 minutes or until just soft.

3. Cut lettuce into 1cm (½in) strips. You should have around 6 cups of packed lettuce in total.

4. Combine all ingredients (except nuts) in a bowl and mix gently.

5. Sprinkle nuts on top.

If you only have whole peanuts you can chop them with a sharp knife or blend briefly in a food processor.

Peanuts

A great garnish or ingredient for any salads. Salad that have peanuts at Revive are usually popular. You can use whole or chopped. Roasted is usually better but raw peanuts are also nice if fresh.

MAKES 7 X 1 CUP SERVES

200g (7oz) 10mm (½in)
rice noodles

2 litres (2qt) water

2 spring onions
(scallions) chopped

2 medium carrots peeled
and grated

optional: 1 cup fresh mung
bean sprouts

1 red capsicum (bell pepper)
finely diced

1 cup freshly chopped
coriander (cilantro)

SATAY SAUCE:

1 large onion roughly chopped

2 tablespoons crushed or
finely chopped ginger

2 cloves garlic finely chopped

2 tablespoons oil

2 teaspoons ground cumin

1 teaspoon ground turmeric

1 teaspoon ground coriander

1 cup peanut butter mixed with
2 cups hot water

1 teaspoon Thai red chilli paste

1 teaspoon salt

4 tablespoons honey or
date puree

This is a great blend of satay sauce, noodles and Thai flavours for that extra zing. You can serve this salad cold, warm or even hot as a meal on its own.

Thai Satay Noodles

1. In a large pot bring the water to the boil. Add rice noodles and cook for 8 minutes or until soft (but not mushy). Rinse in cold water straight away to cool. Drain well.

2. In a pot make the satay sauce. Saute the onion, ginger, garlic and oil until clear. Add spices and then other ingredients, and stir while heating so it is just bubbling. Blend with a stick blender.

3. Combine noodles, vegetables and herbs in a bowl. Pour over the satay sauce and mix gently.

Stainless Steel Bowls

These are great for mixing salads - make sure you have some of different sizes. Extra large ones are great for when you have a crowd. They are relatively inexpensive, light and super easy to clean. Make sure you always select a bigger bowl than you need, mixing is cleaner and more enjoyable.

This would have to be the most requested salad we have at Revive. And the most requested for the recipe. Israeli couscous is more of a pasta than a couscous. Just add some dressing and flavours and it tastes awesome!

Israeli Couscous

MAKES 8 X 1 CUP SERVES

2 cups Israeli couscous

6 cups boiling water

2 cups pumpkin cubed

1 tablespoon oil

¼ cup aioli (page 156)

1 red capsicum (bell pepper) diced

1 cup long green beans cut into 2cm (1in) lengths (fresh or frozen)

3 tablespoons sweet chilli sauce

½ teaspoon salt

1 teaspoon ground turmeric

½ cup finely chopped parsley

1. Put couscous and water in a pot, bring to boil, and simmer with the lid on for around 25 minutes or until soft. Rinse under cold water and drain well.

2. Put pumpkin and oil on a oven tray and bake at 180°C (350°F) for 15 minutes or until soft.

3. Soak the green beans in some boiling water for 2 minutes to take away the raw flavour.

4. Combine all ingredients in a bowl and mix gently.

Israeli Couscous

This is more of a pasta than a couscous. It cooks up into lovely tender small balls that soak up flavours and dressings really well. Cook it like pasta, however it does take around 25 minutes to cook. It is available in most specialty food stores and some supermarkets.

There are a hundred ways to make a roast vegetable salad. This one uses around 50% potatoes which helps keep your prep time and cost down.

Creamy Roasted Veges

MAKES 8 X 1 CUP SERVES

1kg (2lb) white potatoes unpeeled (around 4 large)

2 zucchini (courgettes)

1 red capsicum (bell pepper)

1 large kumara (sweet potato)

4 tablespoons oil

1 teaspoon salt

4 tablespoons sweet chilli sauce

1 tablespoon whole-grain mustard

½ cup aioli (page 156)

garnish: parsley

1. Cut the vegetables into different shapes but keep the size the same, around 2-3cm (1in).

2. Mix vegetables with oil and salt, keeping potatoes separate from other vegetables.

3. In an oven tray, roast the potato for 20 minutes at 180°C (350°F).

4. Add to the tray the remaining faster cooking vegetables (kumara, capsicum, zucchini) and roast all for a further 20 minutes or until soft.

5. Combine all ingredients in a bowl and mix gently.

6. Serve with a sprinkling of freshly chopped parsley.

Let the vegetables cool before mixing or they can go mushy. If you are in a hurry and must use hot vegetables make sure you only mix a couple of times gently with clean hands to avoid mashing everything up.

Capsicum (Bell Pepper)

This vegetable is great for adding colour and we use it extensively at Revive. You can also get pre-diced and frozen capsicum which is great in winter when capsicum is usually very expensive and hard to get. One cup of frozen capsicum is about the same as one fresh capsicum.

So many people were disappointed when this recipe was not included in my first cookbook, so here it is. I will now finally get some peace from Ian and Kaye who can now stop pestering me for it every time they see me! The smoked paprika makes a very flavoursome salad.

Smoked Spanish Rice

MAKES 6 X 1 CUP SERVES

3 cups pre-cooked long grain brown rice (or use 1½ cups rice and 3 cups hot water)

1 cup frozen peas

2 teaspoons smoked paprika

1 teaspoon salt

1 red capsicum (bell pepper) finely diced

½ cup aioli (page 156)

3 tablespoons sweet chilli sauce

1 cup roasted peanuts

1. Cook rice and water with the lid on for 25 minutes (or use pre-cooked rice from your refrigerator).

2. Combine all ingredients in a bowl and mix gently.

This is a great salad to make if you have leftover rice.

I find that the strength of smoked paprika varies considerably between batches and brands so taste first as you may need to add a little more.

Frozen Peas

Always have these in your freezer for an instant green and soothing hit to any salad or hotpot! They do not usually have to be defrosted or cooked, just fire them straight in. Just do not combine with corn and/or cubed carrots or your dish will look like something out of a school cafeteria!

When I travelled in Egypt in 1999 I discovered these little cafe-like Kosharie bars where there are large pans full of rice, pasta, lentils and other things. They serve up this mix with some tomato sauce and that is basically all they sell. This salad is inspired by these bars.

Egyptian Rice & Lentils

MAKES 6 X 1 CUP SERVES

2 cups cooked long grain brown rice (or use ¾ cup rice and 1½ cups hot water)

1 cup French green (puy) lentils

2 grated carrots

1 red capsicum (bell pepper) finely chopped

1 cup frozen peas

½ cup aioli (page 156)

1 teaspoon salt

3 tablespoons sweet chilli sauce

1 teaspoon ground turmeric

garnish: chives

1. Cook rice and water with the lid on for 25 minutes (or use pre-cooked rice).

2. Cook the lentils in plenty of water for around 25 minutes until just soft. Drain well.

3. Combine all ingredients in a bowl and mix gently.

If you cannot find these lentils you can use brown lentils.

French Green (Puy) Lentils

These lentils have green speckled bits on them. They are an excellent lentil as they keep their shape and do not go mushy like most other lentils. Great in salads, casseroles and curries! They take around 25 minutes to cook.

This is a winter dish I put on the menu when lettuce and spinach are expensive and low quality. This salad usually starts off very popular. However after a month interest dies as we find a popular salad will rarely stay popular forever. So I take it off the menu and back on a month later to a great reception!

Thai Bean Mingle

MAKES 6 X 1 CUP SERVES

2 cups broccoli florets

2 cups cauliflower florets

400g (14oz) can red kidney beans drained

100g (3oz) can of bamboo shoots drained

¼ cup aioli (page 156)

4 cups silverbeet (Swiss chard) or spinach ripped

1 red capsicum (bell pepper) diced

2 teaspoons Thai green curry paste mixed with ½ cup water

2 tablespoons honey or date puree

½ teaspoon salt

1.   Cut the broccoli and cauliflower into small florets and cook in some water for around 5 minutes or until just soft.

2.   Combine all ingredients in a bowl and mix gently.

You can use any Thai curry paste (red, yellow, penang, massaman) in this recipe. Add more if you like your food spicier!

Silverbeet (Swiss Chard)

An amazing dark green leafy vegetable. It is one of the few green vegetables readily available through winter. I prefer using it raw in salads to retain its nutrients and size as it cooks down to a very small amount. It is also good to include the crunchy white stalks!

MAKES 4 X 1 CUP SERVES

250g (9oz) 5mm (¼in) rice noodles

3 spring onions (scallions) finely sliced

½ tablespoon salt

½ red capsicum (bell pepper) finely diced

3 tablespoons honey or date puree

3 tablespoons sweet chilli sauce

2 tablespoons soy sauce

1 tablespoon sesame oil

½ cup roasted and salted peanuts finely chopped or blended

2 tablespoons (about 1 stick) lemon grass (fresh or frozen) finely chopped

optional: 4 kaffir lime leaves (fresh or frozen) finely sliced

garnish: 1 cup mung bean sprouts

garnish: 1 cup fresh coriander (cilantro) roughly chopped

We sell this recipe as a salad (cold) at Revive. However it is traditionally a hot main course noodle dish so you can also prepare as such or serve warm!

Pad Thai Noodle Salad

1. Bring some water to boil in a pot and cook the noodles for 8 minutes or until just soft, but not mushy. Rinse and drain well.

2. In a hot pan combine all ingredients (except garnish ingredients) and warm through. This should take no more than 2 minutes.

3. Serve garnished with mung bean sprouts and coriander.

This dish is traditionally served with chicken - however you can also serve this dish with some fried egg strips or tofu on top to make it a complete meal.

You can serve with lemon wedges to squeeze over the noodles.

Sesame Oil

This is a lovely oil that gives a great flavour, often used in Asian dishes. Just sprinkle sparingly over a fresh salad for an extra flavour zing or in any Asian stir fry! Available in most supermarkets.

This is a very easy and delicious way to have potatoes, either hot, warm or cold. It is one of our most raved about recipes. It requires no dressing, just sweet chilli sauce and some parsley.

Bombay Roasted Potatoes

MAKES 5 X 1 CUP SERVES

1kg (2lb) white potatoes unpeeled (around 4 large)

1 teaspoon salt

2 teaspoons ground turmeric

3 tablespoons oil

¼ cup finely chopped parsley

4 tablespoons sweet chilli sauce

1. Cut the potatoes into 2cm (1in) cubes. Do not peel.

2. In a bowl combine potatoes with turmeric, salt and oil and mix well.

3. Place potatoes in a roasting dish and bake for 40 minutes at 180°C (350°F). Half way through cooking mix them so they cook evenly. You want the potatoes to be soft yet still in shape so you may have to adjust cooking time.

4. Combine all ingredients gently in a mixing bowl (reserve half of the sweet chilli sauce and parsley).

5. Put in serving dish and drizzle the remaining sweet chilli sauce and parsley over the top as a garnish.

This is a very popular dish so I recommend you make a double recipe and have some leftovers for lunch the next day.

Salt

Our body needs salt but not in excess. The correct amount of salt is important in any dish. Too much and you can taste it, too little and it is bland. So taste as you go and start with less and add more where necessary!

This is a lovely simple, refreshing undressed salad when mangoes are in season.

Mesclun Mango

MAKES 6 X 1 CUP SERVES

1 mango

100g (3oz) mesclun lettuce mix

½ cup roasted cashew nuts

½ cup dried cranberries

1. Peel the mango, slice off the flesh and cut into strips.

2. Rinse the mesclun in a little water to liven it up and shake well.

3. Combine all ingredients in a bowl and mix gently.

Dried Cranberries

These are a tasty dried fruit that you can add to many salads. Goes well with lettuce and pumpkin. Many are sweetened with sugar so do not consume too many.

I created this salad for our Italian week in 2012. It is a nice colourful blend of ingredients. Pasta is quite easy to make a salad out of, just keep adding vegetables of different colours and a nice dressing and you cannot go wrong.

Italian Fusilli Mingle

MAKES 4 X 1 CUP SERVES

3 litres (3 quarts) water

200g (7oz) wholemeal fusilli (spiral) pasta (around 3 cups)

½ head of broccoli chopped into florets (around 2 cups)

100g (3oz) button mushrooms sliced (around 2 cups)

1 red capsicum (bell pepper) finely diced

1 tablespoon oil

1 teaspoon dried thyme

½ cup aioli (page 156)

1 teaspoon salt

1. Bring water to boil in a pot, add pasta and cook for around 8 minutes or until pasta is al dente (firm but not hard). Drain well.

2. Cook the broccoli in boiling water for around 4 minutes or until just soft.

3. In a small pan saute the mushrooms, capsicum, oil and thyme for around 5 minutes or until soft.

4. Combine all ingredients in a bowl and mix gently.

5. Serve warm or chilled.

Use fresh thyme in this recipe instead of dried if you have access to it. The plants grow very easily.

If you are good with timing you can add the broccoli to the pasta when it is half way through cooking to save on dishes.

Depending on your pasta and vegetables you may like to add a little more aioli.

Wholemeal Pasta

Pasta salads are great, however do not ruin it with white flour based pasta. Hunt out wholemeal varieties which are full of fibre and much better for you. You will also be surprised how good they taste.

I had some friends coming around for dinner and needed something fresh to serve with a curry. In the fridge I had these ingredients, and made this salad in a couple of minutes. Green vegetables are great to have in your fridge and of course are so good for you.

Green Salad & Almonds

MAKES 5 X 1 CUP SERVES

1 large (or 2 small) heads broccoli cut into florets

50g (2oz) baby spinach

1 avocado cubed

½ teaspoon salt

3 tablespoons sesame oil

½ cup sliced almonds

1. Cook the broccoli in some boiling water for around 4 minutes or until just soft.

2. Combine vegetables and salt in a bowl and mix gently.

3. Put in serving dish or on plates and garnish with sesame oil and almonds.

Broccoli

A nice fresh and colourful vegetable that is often served overcooked. You only need to lightly boil or steam it so it is still crunchy. To help retain the green colour put it immediately into cold or iced water after cooking. The stalks are also delicious, just chop off the outside tough layer, dice and cook with the florets!

Quinoa is light, tasty and goes with most vegetables. Use it instead of rice in virtually every way, especially salads. It is four times the price of rice, so make sure you add a lot of ingredients to bulk it out, that way you do not have to use too much. I am notorious for getting distracted when cooking and burning things. Quinoa burns very easily and has an intense smoky smell that permeates the whole house, which have been in trouble for on multiple occasions. So make sure you set a timer when cooking it!

Summer Quinoa Mingle

MAKES 6 X 1 CUP SERVES

½ cup quinoa uncooked

1 cup boiling water

3 cups pumpkin cubed

3 zucchini (courgettes)

1 red onion

1 red capsicum (bell pepper)

2 tablespoons oil

1 teaspoon ground turmeric

2 tablespoons honey or date puree

½ cup chopped parsley

¼ cup lemon dressing (page 156)

1. Cut pumpkin, zucchini, onion and capsicum into cubes, put on an oven tray with oil and cook for 15 minutes at 180°C (350°F) or until soft.

2. Cook quinoa and water with the lid on for 12 minutes or until soft (or use 1½ cup pre-cooked quinoa).

3. Combine all ingredients in a bowl and mix gently.

Small Oven Trays

These are great to have around and I use them all the time. My favourite ones are non-stick, cost under $10, and are around 25 x 35 cm (10 x 15 in) so they fit in the dishwasher! Make sure you get them with a small edge so the food does not slip off. Great when you want to quickly roast some vegetables.

Roasted potatoes + pesto = amazing salad. This is a popular salad when basil is in season. Grow your own basil, make your own pesto and refrigerate or freeze it. There will not be leftovers of this salad.

Pesto Infused Roasted Potatoes

MAKES 6 X 1 CUP SERVES

1kg (2lb) white potatoes unpeeled

2 tablespoons oil

¾ cup basil pesto (page 142)

1 red capsicum (bell pepper) sliced

½ teaspoon salt

1. Cut the potatoes into 2cm (1in) cubes.

2. Put into a roasting dish with oil and bake for 40 minutes at 180°C (350°F). Half way through cooking turn them so they cook evenly. You want the potatoes to be soft yet still in shape so you may have to adjust cooking time.

3. Combine all ingredients in a bowl and mix gently.

Delicious served cold or warm.

Pesto

This delicious mix of basil, nuts, oil and lemon juice can turn average vegetables into heavenly morsels. Great on pasta, potatoes and roasted vegetables. Try making the Revive healthy pesto on page 142.

I created this salad using vegetables from my mother's garden. My mother has an awesome vege garden. You simply pile lots of fresh veges into a bowl and serve up. There are only 3 rules ... colour, colour and colour. Though we do not serve this at Revive, I have included it to show how easy it is to make a fresh green salad.

Wild Green Salad

½ head iceberg lettuce

2 leaves kale

1 large carrot

3 large tomatoes

1 large avocado

6 radishes

20 nasturtium flowers

juice of 1 lemon

1. Wash and slice the lettuce and kale into 2cm (1in) strips.

2. Chop all other vegetables into cubes approximately 2cm (1in).

3. Combine all ingredients in a bowl and mix gently.

4. Garnish with the nasturtiums. Yes you can eat them!

Wash your greens in cold water and dry in a spinner or shake well before using to give them a burst of life and freshness.

Radishes

These give a nice bite and while they are peppery, they have a soothing and freshening effect on any salad.

This salad is exactly as the title says. One day I wanted a fresher chickpea salad so I just made our Greek salad with smaller pieces and added chickpeas!

Greek Chickpeas

MAKES 8 X 1 CUP SERVES

3 tomatoes

½ telegraph cucumber

1 small red onion

150g (5oz) feta cheese

½ cup kalamata olives (pitted)

2 x 400g (14oz) cans chickpeas (garbanzo beans) drained

¼ cup lemon juice

2 tablespoons olive oil

1. Dice vegetables and feta into small pieces about the same size as the chickpeas.

2. Chop the olives in half.

3. Combine all ingredients in a bowl and mix gently.

4. There may be excess juice in the bottom of the bowl from the tomatoes. Drain this before serving.

This salad mainly uses summer vegetables so will be expensive in winter.

If you want this salad dairy free, replace the feta with some lightly fried and salted tofu.

Feta Cheese

We only use the soft cheeses like feta and brie. Hard cheeses like cheddar and parmesan are very difficult for your body to digest. Feta is a strong flavoured cheese and you only need small amounts to add some extra flavour to a dish.

This was a new dish I tried for Italian week in 2012 and it was an instant hit. Cook the pumpkin until it is very soft so it mashes in well with the dressing and rice.

Italian Pumpkin Risotto

MAKES 6 X 1 CUP SERVES

3 cups cooked long grain brown rice (or use 1 cup rice and 2 cups hot water)

3 cups pumpkin cubed

½ cup cashew nuts raw

1 tablespoon oil

½ cup aioli (page 156)

½ teaspoon nutmeg

½ red onion diced

1 teaspoon salt

2 tablespoons honey or date puree

1 teaspoon mixed herbs

1 cup frozen green peas uncooked

1. Cook rice and water with the lid on for 25 minutes (or use pre-cooked rice).

2. Cut pumpkin into 2cm (1in) cubes, put on an oven tray and mix with cashew nuts and oil.

3. Bake for 20 minutes at 180°C (350°F) or until pumpkin is soft.

4. Combine all ingredients in a bowl and mix gently.

Ground Nutmeg

This fragrant spice is excellent with sweet things and pumpkin. Nutmeg has a strong flavour which can overpower a dish, so measure carefully and use sparingly.

This is a colourful and tasty salad I whipped up for Christmas one year. Orange kumara (sweet potato) is very sweet and cooks quickly.

Kumara & Cranberry Mingle

MAKES 7 X 1 CUP SERVES

500g (1lb) orange kumara (sweet potato) unpeeled approx. 2 large

½ teaspoon salt

1 tablespoon oil

2 cups fresh beetroot leaves (pressed down)

1 cup dried cranberries

optional: 50g (2oz) brie cheese

1.   Dice the kumara into 2cm (1in) cubes and mix with the salt and oil.

2.   Place the kumara on an oven tray and bake at 180°C (350°F) for 10-20 minutes or until soft. Let cool slightly.

3.   Combine all ingredients in a bowl and mix gently.

You can use other leafy greens like baby spinach, mesclun or silverbeet (Swiss chard) if you do not have any beetroot leaves.

This salad is also nice with brie cheese cubes on top.

Baby Salad Greens

You can transform a salad with a very small amount of greenery. There are some great pre-packaged greens available like beetroot leaves, rocket and baby spinach. Simply mix in with your salad before serving.

This dish was created in 2012 for our Indian week and is now one of my favourite salads. The peanuts are not noticeable to the eye in this dish as they are a similar size and colour. However it is a great surprise when you eat this salad to discover their hidden flavour and crunchiness.

Curried Black-Eyed Bean Salad

MAKES 5 X 1 CUP SERVES

1 large head broccoli

¼ cup aioli (page 156)

1 teaspoon mild curry powder

2 tablespoons honey or date puree

400g (14oz) can black-eyed beans drained

1 cup frozen peas

1 red capsicum (bell pepper) finely diced

1 cup roasted peanuts

1 teaspoon salt

1. Steam or cook broccoli in some boiling water for around 4 minutes or until just soft.

2. Mix aioli, curry powder and honey together in a cup.

3. Combine all ingredients in a bowl and mix gently.

This salad will work with any white bean variety if you are unable to find black-eyed beans.

Black-Eyed Beans

A lovely soft bean with distinctive black markings. Cooks very quickly and has a unique nutty taste that goes with most vegetables.

Most tabouli is relatively dry and flavourless. However this recipe uses Middle Eastern flavours along with pumpkin for a delicious salad!

Baghdad Bulghur

MAKES 5 X 1 CUP SERVES

1 cup coarse raw
bulghur wheat

2 cups water

3 cups pumpkin cut into
2cm (1in) cubes

1 tablespoon oil

1 head broccoli cut
into florets

1 red onion thinly sliced

1 teaspoon salt

1 teaspoon
ground turmeric

2 tablespoons honey or
date puree

½ cup lemon dressing
(page 156)

1 tablespoon black
sesame seeds

1 tablespoon white
sesame seeds

1. Cook bulghur and water with the lid on for around 25 minutes or until soft.

2. Cut pumpkin into cubes, place on an oven tray with oil and cook for 15 minutes at 180°C (350°F) or until soft.

3. Cook broccoli in some boiling water for around 3 minutes or until just soft.

4. Combine all ingredients (except sesame seeds) in a bowl and mix gently.

5. Garnish with sesame seeds.

Bulghur Wheat (Tabouli)

Bulghur wheat is derived from wheat and has been par boiled so it cooks faster, and is similar to cooking rice. It has a light nutty flavour and is traditionally used in Middle Eastern countries with parsley and called tabouli. It is good to use in salads wherever you would normally use rice.

We have had this salad over the years using different shaped pasta. Though it can be harder to find, try to use wholemeal pasta as it is more nutritious than most pasta which is mainly white flour.

Pesto Penne Pasta

MAKES 5 X 1 CUP SERVES

3 litres (3 quarts) water

200g (7oz) wholemeal penne pasta (around 3 cups)

2 tomatoes

¼ telegraph cucumber

1 small red onion

1 cup basil pesto (page 142)

1. Bring water to boil in a pot, add pasta and cook for around 8 minutes or until pasta is al dente (firm but not hard). Drain well.

2. Finely dice tomatoes, cucumber and red onion.

3. Combine all ingredients in a bowl and mix gently.

4. Taste and add extra salt if required.

Use any wholemeal pasta shape for this recipe like fusilli, macaroni, shells or fettuccine.

Cucumber

A refreshing summer vegetable that goes well in salads. I prefer the telegraph variety as its skin is soft and easy to eat.

This is a lovely way to enjoy the fragrant Thai flavours in a rice salad!

MAKES 6 x 1 CUP SERVES

2 cups cooked long grain brown rice (or use 1 cup rice and 2 cups hot water)

1 stalk celery

1 red capsicum (bell pepper)

1 tablespoon Thai red curry paste

½ cup hot water

½ cup cashew nuts

½ cup cold water

1 cup frozen peas

1 teaspoon salt

2 tablespoons (about 1 stick) lemon grass (fresh or frozen) finely chopped

½ cup fresh coriander (cilantro) roughly chopped

optional: 1 cup roasted peanuts

optional: 6 kaffir lime leaves (fresh or frozen) finely diced

Creamy Thai Rice Salad

1. Cook rice and water with the lid on for 25 minutes (or use pre-cooked rice).

2. Slice celery and dice capsicum.

3. In a cup mix the curry paste with the hot water.

4. Blend the cashew nuts and cold water to form a cashew cream. Use a blender, stick blender or food processor.

5. Combine all ingredients in a bowl and mix gently.

This is a great salad to make if you have leftover rice.

If you like your food a little hotter simply add more curry paste.

Thai Red Curry Paste

This paste is a blend of chilli, spices, ginger, lemon grass and oil and is available in Asian grocery stores and most supermarkets. A small container will last you a long time. Use for an instant Thai flavour hit to any dish. Make sure you mix with a little water so it spreads evenly through your dish.

Many people do not like Brussels sprouts. This is probably because of a bad experience with them. They have an unpleasant flavour when overcooked. They are worth another try if you still have bad childhood memories.

Brussels Sprout Medley

MAKES 6 X 1 CUP SERVES

12 brussels sprouts - ends trimmed and cut in half

3 large carrots cut in half and sliced diagonally

3 stalks celery sliced diagonally

1 red capsicum (bell pepper) sliced into julienne strips

¼ cup aioli (page 156)

½ teaspoon salt

1. Prepare brussels sprouts and cook in boiling water for 4 minutes or until just soft. Drain well.

2. Put carrots on an oven tray with oil and cook for 15 minutes at 180°C (350°F) or until soft.

3. Combine all ingredients in a bowl and mix gently.

Brussels Sprouts

A lovely mini cabbage type vegetable. Halve and steam or boil these for around 4 minutes or until just softened and they are lovely! Do not over cook!

Hotpots & Stir Fries

MAKES 10 X 1 CUP
SERVES

400g pack (14oz) firm tofu

1 onion sliced finely

1 tablespoon oil

2 tablespoons finely
chopped ginger or
ginger puree

2 cloves garlic finely
chopped or crushed

2 tablespoons (about 1
stick) lemon grass (fresh
or frozen) finely chopped

¾ cup peanut butter

2 teaspoons Thai red
curry paste

½ cup warm water

optional: 4 kaffir lime
leaves (fresh or frozen)
finely chopped

1 teaspoon salt

3 tablespoons honey or
date puree

3 cups white cabbage
finely sliced

4 cups water

2 cups chopped 1cm
(½in) pumpkin

200ml (6fl oz)
coconut cream

3 tablespoons
shredded coconut

2 cups green beans
fresh or frozen

garnish: 2 tablespoons
finely chopped roasted
peanuts

garnish: ¼ cup freshly
chopped coriander
(cilantro)

You probably cannot even pronounce "Sadur Lodeh" let alone know what it means. It is usually an Indonesian peanut and chicken curry, so here I have created a Revive version using frozen tofu. It is a delicious curry and now one of my personal favourites!

Indonesian Sadur Lodeh

1. Drain the tofu and slice into strips and put in your freezer for 1-2 days. It will change from being smooth to being rough and stringy. Take out and defrost. Slice into thin strips.

2. Saute onion, oil, ginger, garlic, lemon grass in a pot for about 5 minutes or until clear.

3. Mix peanut butter, curry paste and water into a paste and add to the pot.

4. Add lime leaves, salt, honey, cabbage, water, pumpkin and tofu and simmer for around 20 minutes or until the curry thickens.

5. Stir in remaining ingredients and garnish with chopped peanuts and fresh coriander.

This is a very flavoursome and colourful Mediterranean dish that is usually a side dish. I add chickpeas for some protein so it can be used as a meal on its own.

Classic Chickpea Ratatouille

MAKES 8 X 1 CUP SERVES

1 red onion

3 zucchini (courgettes)

1 large eggplant (aubergine)

3 tablespoons oil

2 cloves garlic finely chopped or crushed

1 red capsicum (bell pepper)

400g (14oz) can chickpeas (garbanzo beans) drained

2 x 400g (14oz) cans chopped tomatoes

1 teaspoon salt

2 tablespoons honey or date puree

garnish: chopped Italian parsley

1. Cut vegetables into 2cm (1in) chunks.

2. Saute red onion, zucchini, eggplant and oil in a large pot, stirring regularly, until eggplant is soft.

3. Add garlic and capsicum and cook for another 2 minutes.

4. Add remaining ingredients, bring to the boil and serve.

Zucchini (Courgettes)

A lovely summer Mediterranean vegetable that adds colour and nice flavour. Can be chopped in many different ways so experiment next time you are using them. Even delicious sauteed on their own.

MAKES 6 X 1 CUP SERVES

2 cups pumpkin diced

1 onion finely sliced

1 tablespoon oil

1 tablespoon finely chopped ginger or ginger puree

2 cloves garlic finely chopped or crushed

2 tablespoons (about 1 stick) lemon grass (fresh or frozen) finely chopped

optional: 6 kaffir lime leaves de-stalked and finely chopped

2 teaspoons ground coriander

4 cups hot water

2 tablespoons honey or date puree

1 teaspoon salt

1 teaspoon Thai green curry paste mixed with 1 cup water

300g (10oz) firm tofu cubed

1 cup frozen peas

1 cup green beans

1 cup chopped mushrooms

1 red capsicum (bell pepper) finely sliced

100g (3oz) can bamboo shoots drained

200ml (7fl oz) coconut cream

garnish: ½ cup freshly chopped coriander (cilantro)

This is another great Thai curry! Green curries are traditionally the hottest, however just go easy on the curry paste if you want something milder. We regularly rotate the different Thai curries around the menu at Revive to keep them interesting.

Thai Tofu Green Curry

1. Cut pumpkin into 2cm (1in) cubes, mix with oil and bake at 180°C (350°F) for 15 minutes or until soft.

2. In a pot saute onion, oil, ginger, garlic, lemon grass and lime leaves for around 5 minutes or until clear. Stir in ground coriander.

3. Add water, honey, salt and curry paste and bring back to the boil.

4. Add tofu, peas, beans, mushrooms, capsicum, bamboo shoots and cook for 5 minutes.

5. Finally stir in pumpkin and coconut cream.

6. Serve with garnish of fresh coriander.

You can substitute other vegetables in this dish if you are missing any, just try to get a good range of colours.

Thai Green Curry Paste

The hottest of all the Thai curry pastes but has a great flavour. Mix with water before using so it spreads evenly through the dish.

I have always loved white creamy mushroom dishes but they usually contain chicken. So here is a Revive healthy version of a dish you would find in Italian restaurants. It is great served over pasta or rice.

Not Chicken Alfredo

MAKES 9 X 1 CUP SERVES

400g (14oz) firm tofu

2 cups pumpkin cubed

1 tablespoon oil

1 onion sliced

2 tablespoons oil

200g (7oz) button mushrooms sliced

1 teaspoon fresh or dried thyme

2 cloves garlic freshly chopped or crushed

1 cup cashew nuts

1 cup cold water

1 red capsicum (bell pepper) sliced

1 yellow capsicum (bell pepper) sliced

3 cups hot water

1 teaspoon salt

2 tablespoons honey or date puree

3 teaspoons arrowroot or cornflour mixed with ½ cup cold water

1. Drain the tofu and put in your freezer for 1-2 days. Take out and defrost. Slice into strips.

2. Bake the pumpkin with oil for 15 minutes at 180°C (350°F).

3. In a pot saute the onion, oil, mushrooms, thyme and garlic for 5 minutes or until soft and mushrooms have reduced.

4. Using a blender or stick blender, blend the cashews and cold water to make a thick cream.

5. Add the cream to the pot with the capsicum, water, salt and honey and simmer for 10 minutes.

6. Add the tofu and pumpkin and simmer for another 10 minutes.

7. Stir in the arrowroot and water mixture to thicken and reheat until thick.

Arrowroot (or Cornflour)

This is a great way to thicken curries and casseroles and soups. It does not work miracles but does assist other components well. Start with 2 teaspoons arrowroot and half a cup of cold water. As it heats it will thicken. However do not add so much that the texture is like glue.

This is a lovely colourful hotpot! Jumbalaya is traditionally a Caribbean meat dish but here is a Revive alternative. You can add any combination of beans you have for this recipe.

Mixed Bean Jumbalaya

MAKES 10 X 1 CUP SERVES

1 large onion diced

2 stalks celery diced

2 tablespoons oil

2 cloves garlic finely chopped or crushed

2 teaspoons smoked paprika

2 x 400g (14oz) cans chopped tomatoes

1 teaspoon salt

3 tablespoons honey or date puree

1 teaspoon chopped chilli or chilli puree

½ cup cashew nuts raw

1 cup water

1 red capsicum (bell pepper) finely diced

1 green capsicum (bell pepper) finely diced

1 cup frozen corn

400g (14oz) can black eye beans drained

400g (14oz) can red kidney beans drained

400g (14oz) can white beans (any variety) drained

garnish: ¼ cup freshly chopped coriander (cilantro) or parsley

1. In a pot saute onion, celery, oil and garlic for 5 minutes or until soft.

2. Add smoked paprika and mix in well.

3. Add the tomatoes. If they are chunky blend them first with a stick blender.

4. Add salt, honey, chilli and cook until bubbling.

5. Blend cashews and water with a stick blender or blender until a fine paste. Add to the pot.

6. Mix in remaining ingredients, and heat so it is just bubbling and serve.

7. Garnish with fresh coriander or parsley.

8. Serve with rice.

You can use a different combination of beans/chickpeas (garbanzo beans) if you like.

We visited Verity's family one night and brought this dish as our contribution for the meal. My brother-in-law, Ryan, really dislikes tofu. After we had finished the meal, everyone wanted to know what was in it and I asked them to guess all of the ingredients. His first guess was "eggs". His jaw dropped as he was very surprised to discover that there were no eggs, he had eaten tofu, thoroughly enjoyed it and declared to his family that he wanted seconds!

Tofu & Quinoa Stir Fry

MAKES 10 X 1 CUP SERVES

2 cups pumpkin chopped into 2cm (1in) cubes

2 carrots finely sliced

1 tablespoon oil

3 cups quinoa pre-cooked (or cook 1 cup quinoa uncooked with 1 cup boiling water)

1 large onion

1 tablespoon ginger finely chopped or ginger puree

3 cloves garlic finely chopped or crushed

2 tablespoons honey or date puree

2 tablespoons oil

2 teaspoons turmeric

600g (20oz) pack firm tofu

1 cup frozen peas

1 red capsicum (bell pepper) finely diced

1 teaspoon salt

1. Mix the pumpkin and carrot with the oil and bake for 20 minutes at 180°C (350°F) or until soft.

2. Simmer quinoa and water with the lid on for 12 minutes or until soft (or use 3 cups pre-cooked quinoa).

3. In a pot saute the onion, ginger, garlic, honey and oil for 5 minutes or until soft.

4. Crumble the tofu into the pot and stir around for a couple of minutes. Sprinkle the turmeric on top and stir in.

5. Add the quinoa, pumpkin, carrot and remaining ingredients.

6. Stir well and cook for around 5 minutes until everything is heated through but not overcooked.

This meal tastes amazing served with hummus!

Turmeric

This lovely ingredient gives a fantastic yellow colour to all it touches. This includes food and also your containers and clothing. It assists with thickening things and has a relatively mild flavour. It is also therapeutically great with anti-inflammatory properties.

This is a great Moroccan version of an Indian dahl with spices and dates! Dates give great sweetness to any dish.

Moroccan Date & Chickpea Dahl

MAKES 8 X 1 CUP SERVES

1 large onion diced

1 tablespoon oil

2 cloves garlic finely chopped or crushed

1 tablespoon finely chopped ginger or ginger puree

1 teaspoon ground turmeric

½ teaspoon ground cinnamon

½ teaspoon ground clove powder

1 cup red lentils

3 cups pumpkin peeled and diced 2cm (1in)

3½ cups hot water

400g (14oz) can chopped tomatoes

400g (14oz) can chickpeas (garbanzo beans) drained

1 cup diced dates

1½ teaspoons salt

garnish: parsley

1. In a large pot saute the onions, oil, garlic and ginger for 5 minutes or until clear.

2. Stir in the spices and heat gently.

3. Add lentils, pumpkin and water, bring to boil and simmer for about 10 minutes or until the lentils and pumpkin are soft. Add extra water if it runs dry before lentils and pumpkin are cooked.

4. Add remaining ingredients and briefly bring back to the boil.

5. Garnish with parsley.

Red Lentils

These lovely lentils are my best friend in the kitchen. Cook these up in under 15 minutes and they go well with virtually anything. Just remember to not add salt until the end as it will inhibit the cooking. Generally you need 3+ cups of water to 1 cup of lentils.

I often cook "freestyle", where I just keep firing available ingredients into a pot. Often it works and I create something delicious, sometimes not. I made this dahl just before the completion of this book and it was delicious, so I knew I had to include it.

Curried Poppy Seed Dahl

MAKES 8 X 1 CUP SERVES

2 orange kumara
(sweet potato) unpeeled

1 tablespoon oil

1 onion diced

2 tablespoons finely
chopped ginger or
ginger puree

1 tablespoon oil

4 teaspoons mild
curry powder

1 teaspoon
ground turmeric

1½ cups red lentils

4 cups boiling water

2 x 400g (14oz) cans
chopped tomatoes

1 teaspoon salt

3 tablespoons honey or
date puree

¼ cup poppy seeds

2 cups frozen peas

200ml (7oz) coconut cream

1. Chop kumara into 2cm (1in) cubes, mix with oil and bake in the oven at 180°C (350°F) for 15 minutes or until soft.

2. Saute onion, ginger and oil for 5 minutes or until soft.

3. Add curry powder and turmeric and mix well.

4. Add lentils and water and simmer for 15 minutes or until lentils are soft. Make sure they do not run out of water and burn.

5. Add the remaining ingredients and the roasted kumara (except coconut cream) and bring up to heat so it is just bubbling.

6. Stir through the coconut cream and serve immediately.

Boiling Water

When preparing a meal the first thing you can do is put the jug on to boil. That way when you come to the part that requires water you have the dish up to a high temperature to start with. You can save at least 5 minutes (sometimes more) by having boiling water on hand.

This is one of our classic Revive favourites. It is a lovely blend of Indian spices in a korma that is very mild.

Indian Spinach & Chickpea Korma

MAKES 7 X 1 CUP SERVES

1 tablespoon brown mustard seeds

2 tablespoons oil

1 large onion chopped

2 cloves garlic finely chopped or crushed

2 tablespoons finely chopped ginger or ginger puree

1 teaspoon ground turmeric

1 teaspoon ground cumin

1 teaspoon ground coriander

1 teaspoon salt

2 x 400g (14oz) cans chopped tomatoes

400g (14oz) can chickpeas (garbanzo beans)

200ml (6fl oz) coconut cream

1½ cups frozen spinach defrosted in hot water and drained

1. In a pot combine the oil and mustard seeds and heat on high heat with the lid on until they start popping.

2. Add the onion, garlic, and ginger and saute for 5 minutes or until soft. Make sure you keep stirring so they do not burn.

3. Add spices and salt and mix well.

4. Add tomatoes and cook until boiling, stirring well.

5. Blend the mixture with a stick blender.

6. Add remaining ingredients and mix in.

7. Serve on rice or couscous.

Add the spinach just before serving. If you leave it in a hot pot too long it will go brown.

Mustard Seeds

These add a delicious nutty flavour to any curry or hotpot. The secret is to cook them at the beginning of the dish on high heat in some oil so they pop open and release their flavour.

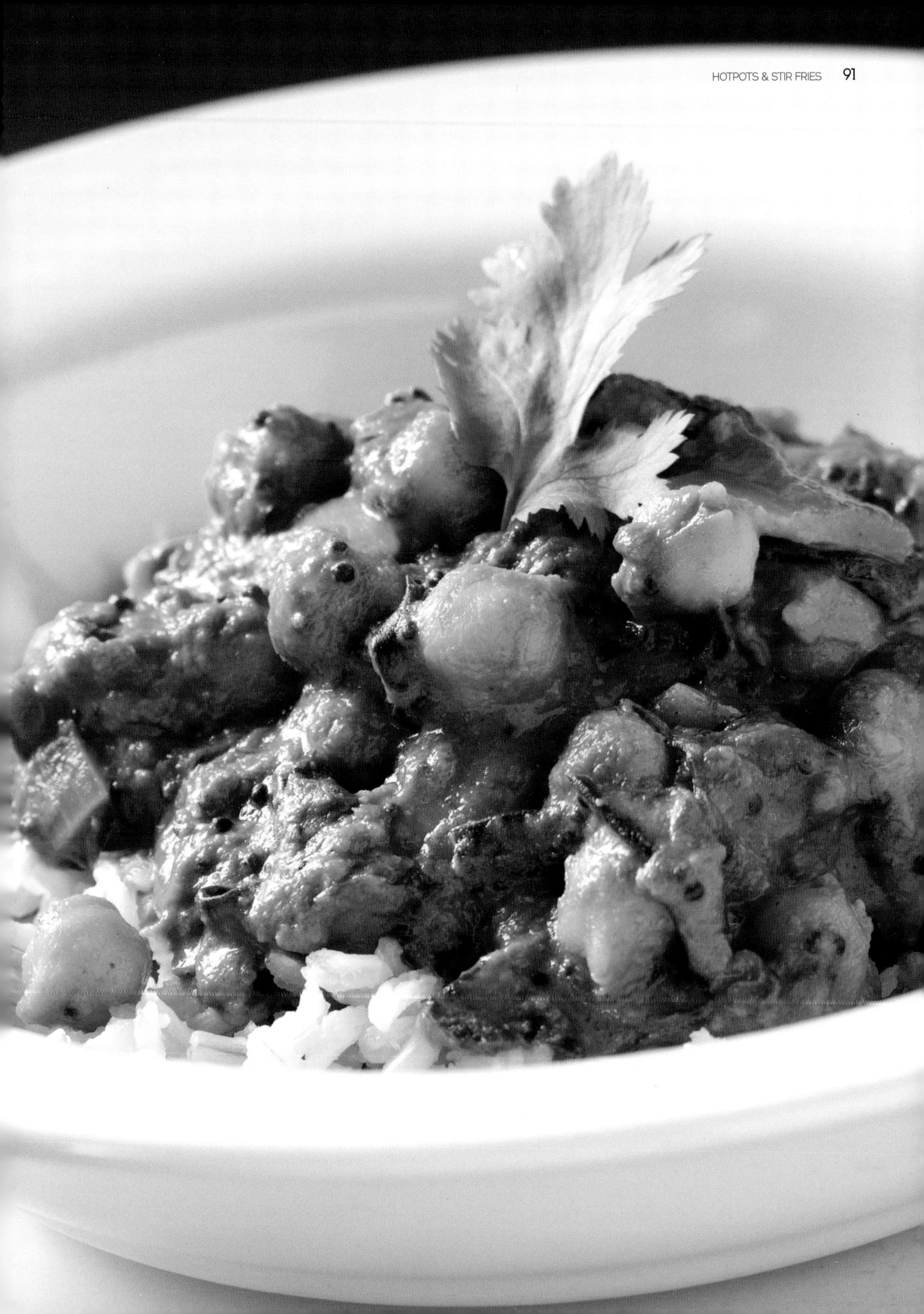

This dish is so simple to make and is delicious and nutritious. You can cook it in under 20 minutes and it does not need any prep or special ingredients!

Tarka Dahl

MAKES 5 X 1 CUP SERVES

1 onion finely chopped

3 cloves garlic finely chopped or crushed

2 tablespoons freshly chopped ginger or ginger puree

1 tablespoon oil

1 teaspoon ground turmeric

1 teaspoon ground cumin

1 teaspoon ground coriander

1 cup dried yellow lentils (toor dahl)

3½ cups boiling water

3 tablespoons honey or date puree

400g (14oz) can chickpeas (garbanzo beans) drained

optional: 200ml (7oz) coconut cream

1 cup frozen peas

1 teaspoon salt

1. In a pot saute the onion, garlic, ginger and oil for 5 minutes or until soft.

2. Mix in the spices and stir briefly.

3. Add the lentils and water, stir and simmer for 15 minutes or until lentils are soft.

4. Stir in remaining ingredients, heat a little and serve.

If you cannot find yellow (toor) lentils then red lentils are fine

Yellow Lentils (Toor Dahl)

These are delicious lentils with a short cooking time. Similar to red lentils but slightly bigger. They are sometimes called toor dahl. However do not get them confused with yellow split peas that are rounder, do not taste all that nice and take much longer to cook.

This is a simple hearty casserole for winter days and nights. Alternatively add some more water and cook longer and you have a soup!

Hearty Lentil Casserole

MAKES 10 X 1 CUP
SERVES

2 medium carrots diced

1 zucchini (courgette) sliced

2 stalks celery diced

2 potatoes cubed

1 large onion diced

2 cloves garlic finely chopped or crushed

1 tablespoon oil

1 cup brown (crimson) lentils

1 teaspoon mixed herbs

4 cups water

3 tablespoons honey or date puree

1 teaspoon salt

2 x 400g (14oz) cans chopped tomatoes

garnish: finely chopped parsley

1. In a pot saute the carrots, zucchini, celery, potato, onion, garlic and oil for 5 minutes or until soft.

2. Add the lentils, mixed herbs and water and cook for around 25 minutes or until soft.

3. Add remaining ingredients and cook for a further 10 minutes.

4. Serve with rice.

Wooden Spoon

There is nothing more soothing than stirring a hotpot with my favourite wooden spoon. Mingling all the ingredients and watching them become a meal is very satisfying. My favourite spoon is quite wide, has a hole in the middle to increase the "stirringness" and pointy edge to get into the corners of pots.

MAKES 4 X 1 CUP SERVES

1 onion sliced

1 tablespoon oil

2 cloves garlic freshly chopped or crushed

2 teaspoons smoked paprika

1 teaspoon ground turmeric

1 teaspoon ground coriander

¼ teaspoon chilli powder

400g (14oz) can tomatoes

½ cup cashews raw

½ cup cold water

1 teaspoon salt

400g (14oz) firm tofu crumbled

400g (14oz) can red kidney beans drained

1 red capsicum (bell pepper) finely diced

2 tablespoons honey or date puree

½ cup freshly chopped coriander (cilantro)

Chilli Con Carne is a meat dish so here is a lovely tofu alternative that is great on corn chips! Just keep adding chilli powder if you want it extra spicy.

Chilli Con Tofu

1. In a pot saute onions, oil and garlic for 5 minutes or until soft.

2. Add spices and chilli and stir in quickly - do not burn.

3. Add tomatoes and bring to boil.

4. Blend with a stick blender until smooth.

5. Make the cashew cream with a blender or stick blender. Blend the cashews and cold water to make a thick cream. Add to the pot.

6. Add remaining ingredients and bring up heat so it is just bubbling.

7. Serve on corn chips or rice.

If you like hot food this is a good recipe to add more chilli!

Chilli Powder

If you like your food a little spicier, a pinch or two of this will add some heat. Just add a little first and taste test as it is not that easy to take out! Be aware that different batches or brands will have different heat levels.

This is a nice potato-based curry with Thai flavourings.

Thai Massaman Peanut Curry

MAKES 6 X 1 CUP SERVES

2 large potatoes unpeeled

½ teaspoon salt

2 tablespoons oil

1 onion diced

2 cloves garlic finely chopped or crushed

1 tablespoon oil

3 tablespoons peanut butter

1 tablespoon massaman curry paste

1 cup hot water

400g (14oz) can black beans drained

100ml (3fl oz) coconut cream

1 teaspoon salt

1 red capsicum (bell pepper) finely sliced

1 cup roughly chopped fresh coriander (cilantro)

½ cup finely chopped roasted peanuts

1. Chop potatoes into 2cm (1in) cubes, mix with oil and salt and bake in the oven at 180°C (350°F) for 30-40 minutes or until soft.

2. Saute onion, garlic and oil for 5 minutes or until soft.

3. Mix peanut butter, curry paste and water to form a paste. Add to the onions and stir in.

4. Simmer for 5 minutes so flavours can mingle.

5. Add remaining ingredients, stir and bring back to heat.

If you cannot find massaman curry paste you can use Thai red curry paste.

Coconut Cream

This is a great cream to add for curries. It is high in fat so go easy. If you want a lower fat version you are better just to use less rather than using the altered "low" or "lite" versions. Make sure you do not excessively heat coconut cream and add at the end of a dish.

MAKES 5 X 1 CUP SERVES

3 cups kumara (sweet potato) cubed unpeeled

1 tablespoon oil

1 onion sliced

1 tablespoon oil

2 cloves garlic finely chopped or crushed

1 tablespoon ginger puree

2 tablespoons (about 1 stick) lemon grass (fresh or frozen) finely chopped

optional: 6 kaffir lime leaves (fresh or frozen)

1 teaspoon Thai green curry paste

5 cups hot water

1 cup raw brown (crimson) lentils

1 teaspoon salt

2 tablespoons honey or date puree

200ml (7fl oz) coconut cream

½ cup freshly chopped coriander (cilantro)

1 red capsicum (bell pepper) diced

If you do not like lentils then you may love this dish. It is our best selling lentil hotpot at Revive.

Thai Green Curry Lentils

1. Chop kumara into 2cm (1in) cubes, mix with oil and bake in the oven at 180°C (350°F) for 15 minutes or until soft.

2. Saute onion, oil, garlic, ginger, lemon grass, lime leaves and curry paste for 5 minutes or until onion is soft.

3. Add water and lentils, bring to the boil, turn down and simmer for 25 minutes or until the lentils are soft. Drain off any water.

4. Add salt, honey and coconut cream and stir until well mixed.

5. Add the roasted kumara and mix. Garnish with coriander and capsicum and serve.

If you are organised and have lentils pre-cooked in your freezer or fridge, you can make this dish quicker by adding these rather than the dry lentils and water.

Heavy Based Pot

A lovely heavy based pot will enhance your cooking experience and is great for hotpots and soups. Just keep piling ingredients in, less chance of burning, and you end up with a great serving container too!

This is a nice simple tomato and bean dish. I love white beans as they have such a moreish and creamy texture.

Italian White Bean Stew

MAKES 6 X 1 CUP SERVES

1 large onion sliced

1 tablespoon oil

4 cloves garlic finely chopped or crushed

1 teaspoon smoked paprika

1 teaspoon dried mixed herbs

2 x 400g (14oz) cans chopped tomatoes

½ cup cashew nuts raw

½ cup water

1 teaspoon salt

3 tablespoons honey or date puree

1 red capsicum (bell pepper) diced

400g (14oz) can large white lima beans (or other white bean variety) drained

1½ cup frozen spinach defrosted in hot water and drained

1. In a pot saute onions, oil and garlic for 5 minutes or until soft.

2. Add smoked paprika and mixed herbs.

3. Add tomatoes and heat until mixture is just bubbling.

4. Using a blender or stick blender, blend the cashews and cold water to make a thick cream. Add to the pot.

5. Add remaining ingredients and heat until it is hot.

6. Garnish with parsley or other fresh herbs.

Cashew Cream

This is a great alternative to cream or coconut milk. Use it anywhere you use milk or cream for a healthier option. Just adjust the amount of water depending on whether you want a milk or a cream.

MAKES 9 X 1 CUP SERVES

2 cups brown
(crimson) lentils

8 cups water

1 large onion finely diced

2 cloves garlic finely
chopped or crushed

1 teaspoon dried
mixed herbs

1 red capsicum (bell
pepper) finely diced

1 yellow capsicum (bell
pepper) finely diced

2 zucchini
(courgettes) diced

2 tablespoons oil

2 x 400g (14oz) cans
chopped tomatoes

¼ teaspoon
cayenne pepper

½ cup raw cashew nuts

½ cup water

2 tablespoons honey or
date puree

1 teaspoon salt

garnish: parsley

Kjirstnne, one of my recipe testers, gave this to her 3 year old nephew Oskar, who is a very fussy eater. He ate it all and requested it for lunch at pre-school. I would not have guessed this recipe would be loved by kids but apparently some do! And adults love it too.

Tuscan Brown Lentils

1. In a medium pot cook the lentils and water uncovered for 25 minutes or until soft. Drain.

2. In another large pot saute the onion, garlic, herbs, vegetables and oil for 5 minutes or until soft.

3. Add the tomatoes and cayenne pepper and heat so it is just bubbling.

4. Using a blender or stick blender, blend the cashews and water into a smooth cream. Add to the tomato mix.

5. Stir in the cooked lentils along with the honey and salt.

6. Simmer and stir for around 5 minutes to let the flavours mingle.

7. Garnish with parsley.

Onions

Onions are a great base for many dishes and are used extensively at Revive. They add sweetness and help round out other flavours. They do need to be sauteed well (not boiled) to make them sweet and tasty. If not, they can make the dish taste like raw onion.

This dish is great served hot, warm or even cold as a salad. The flavours seem to mingle together with time so it tastes great as leftovers the next day.

Asian Peanut Stir Fry

MAKES 6 X 1 CUP SERVES

1 cup sultanas or raisins

3 cups cooked long grain brown rice (or use 1½ cups rice and 3 cups hot water)

4 cloves garlic finely chopped or crushed

2 tablespoons finely chopped ginger or ginger puree

1 large onion sliced

1 red capsicum (bell pepper) diced

2 tablespoons oil

2 tablespoons peanut butter

4 tablespoons water

1 cup peanuts roasted

2 tablespoons honey or date puree

1 teaspoon salt

1 tablespoon sesame oil

2 tablespoons soy sauce or tamari

garnish: 2 spring onions (scallions) finely diced

garnish: ¼ cup white sesame seeds

1. Soak the sultanas in boiling water to soften them up.

2. Cook rice and water with the lid on for 25 minutes (or use pre-cooked rice).

3. In a pan saute the garlic, ginger, onion, capsicum and oil for 5 minutes or until very soft.

4. Drain the sultanas.

5. In a cup mix the peanut butter with the water to form a smooth paste.

6. Add the sultanas, peanut butter paste and all other ingredients (except sesame seeds and spring onions) and stir for a further 5 minutes or until cooked through.

7. Garnish with spring onions and sesame seeds.

This is one of my favourite quick meals to prepare. I always have chickpeas in the freezer and this meal takes me around 5 minutes to cook. I especially love making this dish after I have cooked up a large pot of chickpeas for freezing - there is nothing like the taste of freshly cooked chickpeas!

Mediterranean Chickpea Stir Fry

MAKES 5 X 1 CUP
SERVES

2 tablespoons oil

1 medium purple onion roughly diced

2 tablespoons honey or date puree

2 cloves garlic

1 teaspoon finely chopped fresh ginger or ginger puree

2 large zucchini (courgettes) halved lengthways and then sliced diagonally

1 red capsicum (bell pepper) roughly diced

1 x 400g (12 oz) can chickpeas (garbanzo beans) drained

1 tablespoon black sesame seeds

½ teaspoon salt

3 tablespoons soy sauce or tamari

1. Saute oil, onion, honey and garlic for a few minutes in a pan on high heat to draw out the sweet flavours - do not let garlic burn.

2. Put vegetables in the pan and stir until just cooked but firm, about 4 minutes.

3. Add remaining ingredients and heat through. Check for saltiness and sweetness.

4. Serve with freshly cooked brown rice.

These vegetables are generally good value in summer, so substitute for others in winter.

Soy Sauce

Soy Sauce is a great ingredient to add some saltiness and flavour. You can also use tamari or shoyu which are more natural versions. Look out for flavour enhancers that reside in many soy sauce brands!

This is a simple stir fry with nice fresh flavours. The secret with this one is to cook the vegetables very lightly and let the herbs and caraway seeds do the work.

Herbed Lentil & Quinoa Stir Fry

MAKES 7 X 1 CUP SERVES

½ cup quinoa uncooked

1 cup boiling water

1 cup brown (crimson) lentils

5 cups boiling water

1 large onion finely diced

2 tablespoons oil

2 teaspoons caraway seeds

2 cloves garlic finely chopped or crushed

3 carrots grated

1 red capsicum (bell pepper) diced

1 teaspoon salt

½ cup chopped fresh parsley

¼ cup chopped fresh thyme

1. Simmer quinoa and water with the lid on for 12 minutes or until soft (or use 1 cup pre-cooked quinoa).

2. Cook the lentils in water for around 25 minutes until just soft. Drain well.

3. In a pot saute the onion, oil, caraway seeds, and garlic for 5 minutes or until soft.

4. Add the carrot and capsicum and cook very quickly for 1 minute just to warm them.

5. Mix in the cooked lentils, cooked quinoa and salt and cook for another minute to keep everything warm.

6. Mix in fresh herbs and serve immediately.

Have pre-cooked lentils and quinoa in your fridge or freezer to make this meal very easy and quick to make.

Caraway Seeds

These little seeds contain little bursts of anise-like flavour and is nice in many dishes and in rye bread. Make sure you use them relatively fresh as some pantries can have ten year old herbs and spices floating around. Saute in a little oil to release the flavour.

MAKES 6 X 1 CUP SERVES

3 cups cooked long grain brown rice (or use 1 cup rice and 2 cups hot water)

2 tablespoons oil

4 cloves garlic finely chopped or crushed

1 tablespoon finely chopped ginger or ginger puree

1 large red onion sliced

50g (2oz) button mushrooms finely sliced

1 red capsicum (bell pepper) diced

1 green capsicum (bell pepper) diced

1 stalk celery finely diced

2 spring onions (scallions) finely diced

½ cup cashew nuts roasted

2 tablespoons honey or date puree

1 teaspoon salt

½ cup dates finely chopped

1 teaspoon ground turmeric

2 tablespoons soy sauce or tamari

garnish: fresh coriander (cilantro) and cashew nuts

At Revive we have a variation of this dish as a salad. However at home you can take the time to form it with a cup and use it as a hot meal or side dish.

Indian Rice Pilaf

1. Cook rice and water for 25 minutes with the lid on (or use pre-cooked rice).

2. In a pan, saute the oil, garlic, ginger, vegetables, and nuts for 10 minutes or until very soft.

3. Combine rice, salt, dates, honey and soy sauce with the cooked vegetables.

4. Spoon the mixture into a measuring cup (or normal cup), press down firmly with a spoon and put more in so it is packed tight and level.

5. Tap the cup upside down on the serving plate to release the rice. If it is sticking too much rub a little water or oil in the cup.

6. Garnish with coriander and extra cashews.

You can use a normal cup to make the shapes or use an interesting shaped glass. You can also buy different shaped moulds like pyramids and squares from cooking shops.

Measuring Cups

Make sure you get yourself a good set, preferably stainless steel. When I started cooking I just used approximations. However I now love it when I have a recipe that I can use cups for as I know it will turn out well with only minor intervention. Natural ingredients do change so you still need to try things and adjust.

Main Meals

I love corn fritters and make them at home often. But I needed to find a way to make them work in our cafe where we prepare in the morning and serve from the cabinet over lunchtime. I developed this version which is larger and baked.

Baked Thai Corn Cakes

MAKES 10 CAKES

2 large orange kumara (sweet potato) unpeeled

1 tablespoon oil

1 large onion finely diced

2 cloves garlic finely chopped or crushed

1 tablespoon oil

1 red capsicum (bell pepper) diced small

3 cups frozen whole corn

1 cup chickpea (besan/chana) flour

1 cup freshly chopped coriander (cilantro)

1 tablespoon Thai red curry paste mixed with ½ cup of hot water

1 teaspoon salt

up to ½ cup extra water

oil (for brushing)

1. Cut kumara into 1cm (½in) cubes, put on an oven tray with oil and cook for 15 minutes at 180°C (350°F) or until very soft. Leave the oven on for later use.

2. Saute onion, garlic and oil in a pan for 5 minutes or until the onion is clear. Add the capsicum and corn and saute for another 2 minutes.

3. Combine with all other ingredients in a bowl and mix. The kumara should break up and help bind the mixture.

4. You should have a wet, but sticky mixture. If not you may have to add a little more water.

5. Lightly oil a flat baking tray or use baking paper. Put ½ cup sized cakes on the tray. Brush the top with a light coating of oil.

6. Bake for 30 minutes at 180°C (350°F).

You can use normal red kumara (sweet potato) for this dish if orange kumara is not available or out of season.

Orange Kumara (Sweet Potato)

This is an exceptionally sweet version of the kumara and is amazing in most dishes. It cooks relatively quickly when cut fine and has excellent binding properties so is good for patties like this recipe. This is also sometimes called a Beuregard Kumara.

These are a great alternative to normal burritos. The sweetness of the pumpkin blends really well with the white beans and cranberries.

Tuscan White Bean Wraps

MAKES 6

5 cups peeled pumpkin chopped into 2cm (1in) cubes (approx. ¼ pumpkin)

2 tablespoons oil

1 large onion finely sliced

3 tablespoons honey or date puree

1 tablespoon oil

400g (14oz) can white beans (any variety) drained

½ cup dried cranberries

2 teaspoons ground coriander

½ cup freshly chopped coriander (cilantro)

1 teaspoon salt

optional: 100g (3oz) brie cheese

6 large burritos (tortilla flat bread)

2 tablespoons black sesame seeds

1. Cut pumpkin into cubes, put on an oven tray with oil and cook for 15 minutes at 180°C (350°F) or until soft.

2. In a pan saute the onion, honey and oil for about 5 minutes or until soft.

3. Combine the pumpkin, onion, white beans, cranberries, ground coriander, fresh coriander and salt in a bowl and mix gently.

4. Place 1 cup of the mixture in the middle of a burrito. Bring sides in first and then wrap. Repeat for all 6 wraps.

5. Brush with a little oil and sprinkle the black sesame seeds on top for garnish.

6. Bake for 10 minutes at 180°F (350°F) or until crisp and heated through.

These wraps can be prepared in advance and stored in the refrigerator. Simply pop them in the oven to heat through before serving.

These go well with plum chutney.

White Beans

White beans have a creamy taste that is great! They come in many sizes and names including navy, butter and lima beans. You can usually use them all interchangeably. As with all types of beans, you will get them cheaper and fresher if you soak and cook your own.

We have some sort of frittata on the menu every week at Revive. We just vary the fillings to keep things interesting.

Revive Roast Vege Frittata

MAKES 6 SERVES

1 cup potatoes cubed

1 tablespoon oil

1 cup kumara (sweet potato) cubed

1 cup pumpkin cubed

1 red capsicum (bell pepper) cubed

1 tablespoon oil

2 onions sliced

1 tablespoon oil

8 free range eggs

optional: ½ cup milk or cream

optional: 1 cup cubed feta cheese

½ teaspoon salt

1. Cut vegetables into 2cm (1in) cubes.

2. Put the potato on an oven tray with oil and bake for 15 minutes at 180°C (350°F).

3. Add the faster cooking vegetables (kumara, pumpkin and capsicum) with oil and cook for a further 15 minutes or until all vegetables are soft.

4. In a pan saute the onions and oil for around 5 minutes or until just getting soft.

5. Put the eggs, (milk/cream as desired) and salt in a bowl and mix well with a beater, stick blender or hand whisk.

6. Select a round baking dish approximately 25cm (10in) in diameter.

7. Put the onion mix and roast vegetables in the dish. Pour over the egg mix.

8. Bake at 150°C (300°F) for 20-40 minutes (depending on depth of the mixture and your oven). You want it to be just cooked and not runny. Check by putting a knife in the centre. Cut into wedges to serve.

9. Serve with Revive relish (page 150).

You can add feta cheese on top before you add the egg mix.

Free Range Eggs

Great scrambled, poached, hard boiled and of course, as omelettes and frittatas. Make sure you get free range. Eggs are best eaten in moderation.

This is a great way to have potatoes. We originally called this dish a Greek Kleftali. In researching this recipe book I thought I had better check the spelling and usage, and found that "Keftethes" did exist, however the usage was normally for meatballs! I think one of my chefs must have been playing tricks on me! We now give this dish a more generic name.

Greek Potato & Feta Cake

MAKES 12 X ½ CUP CAKES

1kg (2lb) white potatoes unpeeled (around 4 large)

2 red onions thinly sliced

2 tablespoons oil

½ cup sun-dried tomatoes sliced thinly

3 spring onions sliced

1 cup freshly chopped coriander (cilantro)

100g (3oz) feta cheese cut into small cubes

1 teaspoon salt

1 teaspoon ground cumin

½ cup white sesame seeds

2 tablespoons oil (for frying)

¼ cup chopped parsley

1. Cut potatoes into quarters and put in a pot of boiling water. Simmer until soft (around 10 minutes) and then drain.

2. Mash potatoes roughly so there are still some chunks left.

3. In a pan saute the onion and oil for about 5 minutes or until soft.

4. Combine all ingredients in a bowl (except oil, sesame seeds and parsley) and mix well.

5. Put the sesame seeds on a plate.

6. Measure out ½ cup of the potato mix and roll into a ball with your hands. Roll in the sesame seeds so it is liberally covered. Repeat with remaining potato mixture.

7. Heat a non stick frying pan with a little oil. Fry cakes for around 3 minutes each side or until lightly brown. Sprinkle with parsley and serve.

You can also cook these in the oven if you do not want to spend time flipping. Simply brush with oil and bake for 20 minutes at 150°C (300°F).

These are great served with Revive Relish (page 150) and a green salad.

Ground Cumin

This delicious spice usually goes in curries. However it is also great added in small quantities to many dishes and helps round off flavours of some dishes even though you would not know it is there.

MAKES 8 SERVES

3 large potatoes

1 teaspoon salt

½ cup soy or rice milk

3 cups pumpkin 2cm (1in) cubes

1 tablespoon oil

1 medium onion sliced

1 tablespoon oil

1 tablespoon finely chopped ginger or ginger puree

2 cloves garlic finely chopped or crushed

2 tablespoons (about 1 stick) lemon grass (fresh or frozen) finely chopped

1 teaspoon Thai red curry paste mixed with ¼ cup warm water

400g (14oz) can chopped tomatoes

1 tablespoon arrowroot (or cornflour) mixed with 1 tablespoon cold water

1 teaspoon ground coriander

1 teaspoon ground turmeric

¼ cup fresh coriander (cilantro) chopped

300g (11oz) pack of firm tofu cut into 1cm cubes

1 red capsicum (bell pepper) diced

1 teaspoon salt

2 tablespoons honey or date puree

100ml (3fl oz) coconut cream

6 large sheets filo pastry approx. 100g (3oz)

A recent discovery at Revive that is a cross between a Thai curry and a shepherd's pie. It is one of my new favourites. The recipe may look daunting - however it is just a curry mix and a mashed potato mix.

Thai Tofu Curry Pie

1. Cut potatoes into quarters and put in a pot of boiling water. Simmer until soft (around 10 minutes) and then drain. Add salt and milk and mash well.

2. Cut pumpkin into cubes, put on an oven tray with oil and cook for 20 minutes at 180°C (350°F) or until soft.

3. In a pot, saute onion, oil, ginger, garlic and lemon grass until soft. Then add remaining ingredients (except coconut and filo) and bring back to boil. Stir in coconut cream. The pumpkin should break up to thicken the mixture.

4. Select a baking dish around 20 x 30 cm (8 x 12 in) in size.

5. Put 6 layers of filo pastry in an oiled oven dish with the edges hanging over the side of the dish. Lightly brush oil between each layer. If your filo is smaller than the dish you may have to have 2 sheets per layer.

6. Pour in curried tofu mix which should be quite thick.

7. Add potato mash on top. Roll and fold the hanging filo around to form a crust inside the tray. Brush oil over the filo.

8. Bake at 150°C (300°F) for 30 minutes.

Lemon Grass

This is a lovely Thai flavour. You can buy lemon grass in stalks and just chop finely. Or it is very convenient buying a pack of frozen lemon grass from your local Asian supermarket and keeping it in your freezer. You can buy frozen stalks or even packs of frozen lemon grass pre-chopped.

SERVES 6

3 cups white cashew
sauce (page 152)

6 cups Italian tomato
sauce (page 157)

1 cup brown
(crimson) lentils

1 teaspoon sage

½ teaspoon salt

2 cups pumpkin sliced

2 cups kumara (sweet
potato) sliced

1 red capsicum
(bell pepper)

2 tablespoons oil

½ teaspoon salt

2 onions

2 tablespoons oil

2 tablespoons honey or
date puree

6 large fresh wholemeal
lasagne sheets (or
use dried and soften in
boiling water for
3 minutes)

garnish: ¼ cup pumpkin
seeds and
chopped parsley

The classic vegetarian dish. However, some lasagnes are dripping in cheese so I wanted one that was more wholesome and actually healthy. This may look like lots of steps (and it is) but it is just preparing the different components and layering together. Many steps can be done in advance in bulk and stored in your freezer or fridge.

Lentil & Vegetable Lasagne

1. Make white cashew sauce and tomato sauce if you do not already have them in your fridge or freezer.

2. Cook lentils with 3 cups water for 20-30 minutes or until soft. Drain and mix with the salt and sage.

3. Cut pumpkin and kumara into thin slices. Slice red capsicum. Put on an oven tray mixed with the oil and saltand cook for around 15 minutes at 180 °C (350°F) or until just soft.

4. Saute onion, oil and honey in a pan for around 5 minutes or until soft.

5. Select a deep baking dish approx. 20 x 30 cm (8 x 12 in). Pour 1 cup tomato sauce in dish, place lasagne sheets, then 1 cup tomato sauce, and cooked lentils and half the cashew sauce.

6. Add another layer of lasagne sheets and then add roast vegetables. Cover with remaining tomato sauce. Add remaining lasagne sheets and cover with white cashew sauce.

7. Bake for around 40 minutes at 180°C (350°F).

8. Garnish with freshly chopped parsley and pumpkin seeds.

Parsley

A quick dusting of some finely chopped parsley can sometimes give a dish that bit of green it needs. It is so easy to grow so make sure you plant a whole lot in your garden (or in pots) each spring. It is however a food crime to put large sprigs of parsley on any food.

These are easy to whip up for a quick accompaniment for a special meal or a light dinner.

Curried Potato Cakes

MAKES 12 CAKES

500g (1lb) potatoes (around 2 medium)

1 large onion
finely chopped

½ cup chickpea (besan/chana) flour

2 teaspoons curry powder

1 teaspoon salt

½ cup soy or rice milk

2 tablespoons honey or date puree

½ cup chopped parsley

2 tablespoons oil for frying

1. Chop potatoes and boil in water for around 5-10 minutes or until soft. Drain and mash lightly so there are still soft chunks of potato.

2. Combine all ingredients in a bowl and mix well.

3. Heat a non-stick fry pan and add a little oil.

4. Take out 2 tablespoon scoops and press down into the pan. Fry for around 1 minute per side.

5. Serve with tomato sauce, chutney or salsa.

When I fry fritters or cakes I always do one first and then adjust temperature or mixture so the rest turn out perfect.

Soy, Almond & Rice Milk

Milks are great to use when liquid is required but a thicker and creamier texture is needed. You can make your own milks. See page 166 for the recipe for almond milk!

I saw a similar meal in a pie shop one day so thought I would customise something healthier for Revive. Filo is quick to work with and crisps up well.

Indian Curried Filo Pie

MAKES 8 X 1 CUP SERVES

3 cups pumpkin chopped into 1cm (½in) cubes

3 cups potato chopped into 1cm (½in) cubes

½ teaspoon salt

2 tablespoons oil

1 large onion sliced

1 tablespoon finely chopped ginger or ginger puree

2 cloves garlic finely chopped or crushed

1 tablespoon oil

1 teaspoon ground turmeric

1 teaspoon ground cumin

1 teaspoon ground coriander

2 x 400g (14oz) cans chopped tomatoes

1 cup frozen peas

1 red capsicum (bell pepper) finely chopped

200ml (6fl oz) coconut cream

1 teaspoon salt

400g (12oz) can chickpeas (garbanzo beans) drained

150g (5oz) filo (very fine) pastry

oil for brushing

1. Put pumpkin and potato in a roasting dish with salt and oil and bake at 180°C (350°F) for 30-40 minutes or until potato is just cooked and pumpkin is very well cooked.

2. In a pot, saute onion, ginger, garlic and oil until clear.

3. Mix in spices and stir briefly. Add tomatoes and bring to the boil.

4. Add roasted pumpkin and potato, red capsicum, peas, coconut cream, chickpeas and salt to the pot and mix gently.

5. Select a deep oven tray approx. 20 x 30 cm (8 x 12 in).

6. Layer filo on the bottom, up the sides and hanging over the edge. Brush a little oil, repeat for 6 layers.

7. Pour in the curry mix.

8. Add 3 layers of filo pastry on top. Roll the overlapping filo together to form a crust inside the dish. Make sure there is a good brushing of oil on top.

9. Bake at 150°C (300°F) for approximately 30 minutes.

10. Garnish with parsley or another green herb.

11. Cut into squares and serve with a fresh salad.

Work with filo pastry quickly so it does not dry out. If you get interrupted, roll it up and put back in the refrigerator.

If you like your food hotter you can add some chilli or chilli paste to the mix to spice it up a bit.

I love the challenge of making something unhealthy healthy. One Saturday night with some friends we wanted pizza but did not want anything unhealthy. So I whipped this up with a chickpea bread base and some delicious toppings I had in the fridge. A friend of ours, Dawn, is a pizza connoisseur so I was very happy when she said she thought it was delicious and would make it herself!

Chickpea Pizza

MAKES 12 PIECES TO SERVE 6 PEOPLE

3 cups chickpea (besan/chana) flour

3 cups water

1 teaspoon onion powder

½ teaspoon garlic powder

2 tablespoons oil

1 teaspoon salt

oil for brushing the tray

2 medium onions thinly sliced

1 teaspoon oil

2 cups Italian tomato sauce (page 157)

4 cups spinach chopped into small pieces

½ red capsicum (bell pepper) sliced thinly

1 cup hummus

12 black olives pitted

1. In a mixing bowl, combine the chickpea flour with 1 cup of the water and mix well. When mixed, slowly add the rest of the water while mixing. This process will help avoid clumps.

2. Add the onion powder, garlic powder, oil and salt and mix well.

3. Select an oven tray (with sides) around 300 x 400mm (12 x 16in). Brush well with oil.

4. Pour in the chickpea mix and bake at 180°C (350°F) for 15 minutes. The mixture may seem to be too runny however this is normal.

5. In a small frying pan, saute the onion and oil until soft and brown.

6. Warm up the tomato sauce.

7. On top of the pizza base start with the tomato sauce and then layer on the caramalised onion, the spinach and capsicum.

8. Add dollups of hummus with olives placed on top.

This needs to be eaten straight away or the tomato sauce will leak through the base. If you need to eat later - just prepare the ingredients and add the toppings just before serving.

Black Olives

Generally we use Kalamata Olives at Revive, however black olives are a nice olive too with a more subtle olive taste. We always buy our olives pitted for fast usage and to avoid stones. The dark colour of olives contrasts well in most dishes.

Burger patties are usually very quick to make, and these are a complete protein having brown rice and lentils. The rice flour is the key binding agent in this recipe.

Beefless Burgers

MAKES AROUND 15 SMALL BURGER PATTIES

½ cup brown (crimson) lentils

2 cups water

1 onion sliced and lightly fried

1 cup cooked brown rice

¼ cup rice flour

2 tablespoons sweet chilli sauce

½ teaspoon ground turmeric

1 tablespoon soy sauce

¼ teaspoon salt

4 tablespoons savoury yeast flakes

¼ cup water

oil for frying

1. Cook lentils and water for around 30 minutes or until soft.

2. Saute onion and oil in a pan for around 5 minutes or until soft.

3. Mix all ingredients well in a bowl and let sit for around 5 minutes.

4. Fry in a hot non-stick fry pan with a little oil - around 2 minutes per side.

5. Serve with vegetables or with a fresh wholemeal bun and salad.

Make a double batch and freeze for instant burgers in your freezer.

With any mixture that requires holding together ensure the mix is sticky. If not, add a little more flour, or a little more water to get the right texture. Often recipes like this will hold together on standing as the moisture permeates all of the ingredients.

Rice Flour

This is a great binding ingredient to use with burger patties or fritters. It has no taste and is gluten free.

This is another variation on our cannelloni to keep things interesting. It is a great combination of ingredients and the sweet pumpkin and cranberries contrast well with the tomato sauce.

Tuscan White Bean Cannelloni

MAKES 10

2 cups pumpkin

1 large onion sliced

1 tablespoon oil

1 tablespoon oil

400g (14oz) can white beans (any size) drained

½ cup freshly chopped coriander (cilantro)

½ cup dried cranberries

2 tablespoons honey or date puree

300g (11oz) firm tofu mashed

1 teaspoon dried thyme

1 teaspoon salt

5 fresh wholemeal lasagne sheets (or use dried and soften in boiling water for 3 minutes)

4 cups Italian tomato sauce (page 157)

garnish: finely chopped parsley

1. Cut pumpkin into ½cm (¼in) slices, put on an oven tray with oil and cook for 15 minutes at 180°C (350°F) or until soft.

2. Saute onions and oil in a pan for 5 minutes or until soft.

3. In a bowl combine all ingredients except for pasta sheets and tomato sauce.

4. Cut pasta sheets into strips so they measure approximately 10 x 20 cm (4 x 8 inches). Lay them out on your bench.

5. Place ½ cup of the mix in the middle of a pasta strip. Fold the side closest to you over the top, and roll on the remaining piece. Repeat for the remaining cannelloni.

6. Spread 1 cup Italian tomato sauce over the base of an oven tray. Place the cannelloni gently in the tray. Cover liberally with the remaining sauce.

7. Bake at 150°C (300°F) for 40 minutes.

Lasagne sheets come in all different shapes and pack sizes so plan out your sheets when you purchase them.

These are great with some feta cheese sprinkled on top in the last 5 minutes of cooking.

This is a classic dish (healthy version) that you can whip up anytime at home! The sweet chilli sauce and fresh coriander are the secret ingredients to make them taste amazing!

Traditional Corn Fritters

MAKES 10 LARGE FRITTERS

1 medium onion finely diced

1 tablespoon oil

2 cups frozen or canned whole kernel corn (no need to defrost if frozen)

1 cup chickpea (besan/chana) flour

up to ½ cup water

1 teaspoon salt

3 tablespoons sweet chilli sauce

½ cup freshly chopped coriander (cilantro)

oil (for frying)

optional: salsa made from tomato, avocado, red onion and coriander (cilantro)

1. Saute the onion and oil until soft.

2. Mix all the ingredients together in a mixing bowl. You may need to add up to an extra half a cup of water to achieve a thick paste.

3. Let the mixture sit for around 20 minutes in the fridge, then stir again. If you are in a rush this is not absolutely necessary but you will end up with a more consistent mix that will stick together better.

4. Fry ¼ cup scoops with a little oil in a hot pan (ideally non-stick). Cook for around 3 minutes each side or until golden brown.

5. Serve immediately with salsa on top.

You can use wholemeal flour instead of chickpea flour in this recipe.

When making fritters I make a test one first to check consistency, the heat of the pan and that everything sticks together.

Non-Stick Frying Pan

Having a light non-stick frying pan is very handy. They heat up quickly, you do not need much oil and you can throw them straight in the dishwasher when finished. Great for sauteing onions or small components of a dish.

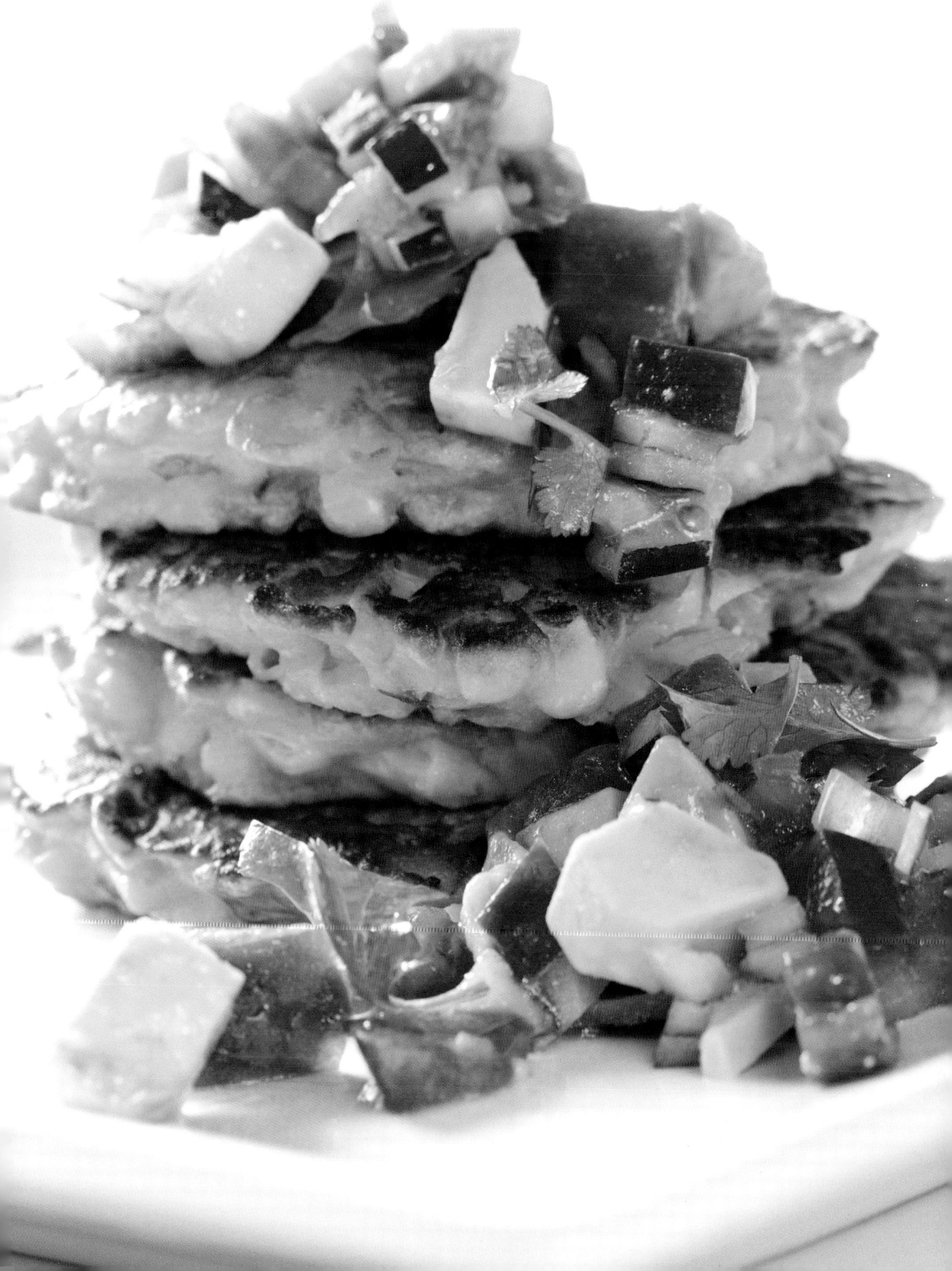

Flavour Boosters

Pesto is an amazingly flavourful dip or sauce that goes with so many things. It is very expensive to buy, yet very inexpensive to make - especially if you grow your own basil. This is a healthier pesto recipe without cheese and too much oil.

Healthy Basil Pesto

MAKES 2 CUPS

1 large bunch fresh basil
(around 125g/4oz)

½ cup rice bran oil

1 cup cashew nuts

½ teaspoon salt

¼ cup lemon juice
(2 lemons)

2 cloves garlic

1. Put all ingredients into a food processor and blend until it is well mixed, but there are still some nut pieces showing.

2. You can use a blender or stick blender but you will have to add a little more oil or water to make the mixture turn.

For a different flavour you can use almonds or walnuts instead of cashew nuts.

Traditionally pesto uses pine nuts - however these are around 4 times the price of almonds and cashews.

Fresh Basil

The most incredible smell and flavour comes from fresh basil. Great in salads, dips and as a garnish. It goes black when it gets hot so only use in cold applications.

While not technically a "flavour enhancer", this bread is a great accompaniment to any meal. It contains protein due to the chickpea (besan/chana) flour and very tasty. Chick Bread is great served with curries or any tomato stew. Chickpea flour is available at any Indian or health store. Keep the ingredients for this recipe on hand so you can make it at any time.

Chick Bread

MAKES 4-6 SERVES

1½ cups chickpea (besan/chana) flour

1½ cups water

¾ teaspoon salt

1 tablespoon oil

1 teaspoon mixed herbs

1 teaspoon onion powder

½ teaspoon garlic powder (or 2 cloves garlic finely chopped or crushed)

1. In a mixing bowl, combine chickpea flour with a little of the water so you have a thick paste.

2. Add remaining water and ingredients and mix well.

3. Lightly oil a non-stick baking tray with sides, ideally around 25cm x 30cm (10 x 12 inches).

4. Pour mixture into the tray - it will be quite runny - this is normal.

5. Bake for 15 minutes at 180°C (350°F).

6. Let cool and carefully slice into slabs.

7. Garnish with some fresh herbs and eat immediately.

Resist the temptation to mix all the water in first as this will cause you to have lumps in the mixture.

This is a great base for pizzas!

Onion Powder

This is something that can add body to dishes if you do not have onions available. It is quite strong so it needs to be used in moderation. Start with ½ teaspoon where you would normally have 1 medium onion.

Great on many meals and salads, guacamole is quick to make and you will never have any left over. Make sure you make it fresh as it will not keep very well.

Avocado Guacamole

MAKES 1-2 CUPS

1 large or 2 medium avocados (ripe)

1 small tomato finely diced

¼ red onion finely diced

1 clove garlic chopped or crushed

2 tablespoons freshly squeezed lemon juice

¼ teaspoon salt

optional: 2 tablespoons sweet chilli sauce

1. Halve, carefully remove the stones and skin of the avocado and put in a mixing bowl. Mash with a fork.

2. Add all other ingredients and mix together.

I prefer not too much onion and tomato in my guacamole, however if you want more texture put in more onion and tomato.

Avocado

A beautiful ingredient and awesome as guacamole. Sliced up will transform many meals or salads. Take care if you extract the stone with a knife as apparently it is one of the most common causes of kitchen accidents.

I love the colour of this dip. Roasted beetroot has an amazing sweet flavour and makes a nice dip.

Root-beet Dip

MAKES 2 CUPS

2 medium beetroot

1 tablespoon oil

400g (14oz) can chickpeas (garbanzo beans) drained

½ cup roasted or raw cashew nuts

2 tablespoons tahini (sesame seed paste)

3 tablespoons lemon juice

½ teaspoon salt

1 clove garlic

1 teaspoon ground cumin

up to ½ cup of water if needed

garnish: parsley

1. Peel the beetroot and chop into cubes. Put on an oven tray and mix with the oil. Bake for 40 minutes at 180°C (350°F) or until soft.

2. Put all ingredients in food processor and process until smooth. You can also use a stick blender.

3. Taste and add more water, salt or lemon juice if required.

4. Garnish with some finely chopped parsley.

5. Serve with corn chips, rice crackers and/or vegetable sticks.

A delicious dip for chips or raw vegetables. Or use as a tasty garnish on top of fritters or other meals.

Red Pepper Pesto

MAKES 2½ CUPS

2 red capsicum
(bell peppers)

1½ cups raw nuts
(cashews and/or almonds)

½ teaspoon salt

¼ cup oil

2 cloves garlic

up to ¼ cup water

1. Cut the capsicum into quarters and remove the seeds. Put on an oven tray with the nuts and a little oil.

2. Bake for 20 minutes at 150°C (300°F).

3. Combine with remaining ingredients into a food processor and blend until it is well mixed, but there is still some nut pieces showing for texture.

4. You may need to add a little water to achieve desired consistency.

You can make this recipe quicker and with a more "raw" taste by not roasting the nuts and capsicum.

This will store in your refrigerator for around 2 weeks if kept covered.

We serve this relish with our frittatas at Revive. It is so easy to make your own relishes and they taste fresher than store-bought options.

Revive Relish

MAKES 3 CUPS

2 large onions sliced

1 teaspoon mustard seeds

1 tablespoon oil

1 teaspoon chopped chillies or chilli puree

2 tablespoons honey or date puree

1 teaspoon curry powder

½ teaspoon clove powder

1 teaspoon salt

½ cup sultanas

2 apples cored and roughly chopped

2 x 400g (14oz) cans chopped tomatoes

1½ tablespoons apple cider vinegar

1. Put onion, oil, mustard seeds into a pot and saute.

2. Stir until mustard seeds start to pop and onion is soft.

3. Add all other ingredients.

4. Bring to boil, turn down and simmer on very low heat for 1 hour.

5. Blend with a stick blender.

Will keep in the fridge for around a month. Alternatively you can freeze or bottle in preserving jars.

Chillies

Not only can chillies add heat to food, but they can help round out flavours too. Make sure you add sparingly. You can buy chilli puree (also called crushed chilli) in supermarkets which is great to have in the fridge ready to use when you need it.

This is a healthier white sauce that you can use in lasagnes and over steamed vegetables.

White Cashew Sauce

MAKES 4 CUPS

1½ cup cashew nuts raw

1 cup cold water

1 large onion sliced

2 tablespoons oil

2 cups hot water

1 teaspoon salt

2 teaspoons whole-grain mustard

1 tablespoon tapioca flour (can also use cornflour or arrowroot)

2 tablespoons cold water

1. Blend cashews and water in blender to make cashew cream.

2. In a pot saute onion and oil for 5 minutes or until soft.

3. Add hot water, salt, whole-grain mustard and cashew cream. Bring to boil, stirring regularly.

4. In a cup, mix tapioca with cold water and add to pot.

5. Blend with a stick blender to make a smooth sauce.

6. Simmer on low heat for around 5 minutes or until thick. Stir regularly.

You can use cashew pieces instead of whole cashews for this as they are cheaper.

*This salsa is bursting with flavour and will be a great
addition to any meal. Great to dip corn chips into too!*

Tomato Salsa

MAKES 3 CUPS

4 large ripe tomatoes

1 yellow capsicum
(bell pepper)

1 red capsicum
(bell pepper)

2 spring onions (scallions)

1 small red onion

¼ cup lemon juice

½ teaspoon salt

½ cup chopped fresh
coriander (cilantro)

1.   Chop up the vegetables into small pieces and put in a mixing bowl.

2.   Add lemon juice, salt and coriander and mix well.

This salsa is best made fresh. If you do need to prepare ahead of
time chop the vegetables and put in the fridge with cling wrap. Add the
lemon juice and salt just before serving.

This is a great alternative to hummus when you want something different.

Ravishing Red Bean Dip

MAKES 4 CUPS

1 clove garlic

½ teaspoon salt

2 x 400g (14oz) cans red kidney beans drained

2 teaspoons smoked paprika

2 tablespoons oil

4 tablespoons tahini (sesame seed paste)

4 tablespoons lemon juice

½ cup walnuts

¾ cup water

1. Put all ingredients into a food processor, or use stick blender. Note that normal blenders do not usually work as dips are too thick.

2. Process for around 1 minute or until fully processed and smooth. You may need to add extra water.

3. Taste and check for saltiness, lemon-ness and smoked taste (note all of these ingredients vary significantly so some taste is needed here).

4. Serve with vegetable sticks, corn chips or rice crackers.

Will keep in the fridge for around a week (ensure you use very clean implements and chill immediately if you wish to keep longer than a couple of days).

Tahini (Sesame Seed) Paste

This is made from crushed roasted sesame seeds. It has the consistency of runny peanut butter. Tahini adds great consistency and flavour to dips and sauces. Try using tahini on toast instead of peanut butter!

Revive Aioli

MAKES 3 CUPS

½ cup soy milk

1 tablespoon cider vinegar

3 cloves garlic

1 tablespoon whole grain mustard

½ teaspoon salt

2 cups oil

½ to 1 cup room temperature water

1. Select a blender, food processor or stick blender.

2. Blend all ingredients (except oil and water).

3. While blending, slowly add oil and then add water at end until desired consistency is reached.

When making dressings you need to ensure that all items are at room temperature, and that you add the oil slowly.

Lemon Dressing

MAKES 1 CUP

½ cup oil

2 cloves garlic crushed

1 teaspoon ground cumin

1 teaspoon salt

½ cup lemon juice

1. Select a blender, food processor or stick blender.

2. In a cup or jar mix all ingredients together.

You can just mix this dressing by hand if you do not have a blender.

Italian Tomato Sauce

MAKES 6 CUPS

1 large onion

4 cloves garlic crushed

2 tablespoons oil

3 x 400g (14oz) cans tomatoes

¾ teaspoon salt

1 teaspoon mixed dried herbs

3 tablespoons honey or date puree

1. In a pot saute onion, garlic and oil until clear.

2. Add remaining ingredients and cook until bubbling.

3. Blend all of the sauce with a stick blender.

If you really like garlic add 2 times as much for a great garlic taste.

Date Puree

MAKES 2 CUPS

2 cups pitted dried dates

2 cups boiling water

1. Put dates in boiling water for 5 minutes to soften.

2. Put all water and dates in blender and blend well until you have a smooth paste.

3. If you hear date stones (as they occasionally come through), sieve the puree.

4. Put into an air-tight container and store in the refrigerator. Will last at least 3 weeks.

You can use cold water to soak the dates - however it will take several hours for them to soften.

THE RECIPES ON THESE PAGES HAVE BEEN REPEATED FROM MY FIRST BOOK, "THE REVIVE CAFE COOKBOOK"

Sweet Things

We used to make these at Revive when we first started and they were very popular but as we sold so many they were time consuming for us to make. Phil, a good friend of mine who is an engineer, said he could design a machine to make them. So we teamed up and now we sell a similar product to hundreds of retailers under the name "Frooze Balls" in 3 flavours (original, apricot and banana). But if you still want to make your own here is the recipe!

Bliss Balls

MAKES 12 BALLS

½ cup dried dates

½ cup dried apricots

½ cup cashew nuts

½ cup almonds

3 tablespoons carob powder

½ cup water (or less)

½ cup shredded coconut

1. Soak fruit in boiling water for around 5 minutes. This is not essential but will soften the fruit and help your food processor last longer.

2. Put fruit, nuts, carob and half the water into a food processor and blend until you have a consistent paste.

3. Add water as needed so you get the balance between a mix that will blend and one that is not too soft.

4. Pour coconut on a plate.

5. Spoon out ¼ cup and divide into two so you have eighth cup size balls. Roll each into circular balls in your hands and put in the coconut. It is best to do all the rolling together while your hands are sticky.

6. Wash and dry your hands and mix carefully in the coconut.

7. They will harden up a little when you refrigerate them.

Blending fruits and nuts can put extra stress on your food processor so if you do double mixes blend in 2 batches.

You can choose your size and make large or very small balls.

Carob Powder

Carob powder is a naturally occurring sweet flavouring. It is similar to cocoa powder, except that it is sweeter and not bitter. It does not contain caffeine and is much better for you. It is available at most natural health stores.

I usually have 5 grains for breakfast, however I sometimes like something else. So one day I pulled out an old Revive muesli recipe (when we used to serve breakfasts) and made this up. Some muesli recipes insist you cook for two hours - however this one is done in 20 minutes and tastes great. You will also save a lot as this is cheaper than store bought muesli.

Revive Muesli (Granola)

MAKES 4 CUPS

1 cup rolled oats whole

1 cup rolled oats fine

½ cup shredded coconut

3 tablespoons sesame seeds

3 tablespoons sliced almonds

3 tablespoons cashew nut pieces

3 tablespoons sunflower seeds

4 tablespoons liquid honey or date puree

4 tablespoons oil

¼ cup sultanas

optional: ½ cup other dried fruit of your choice
 - dates
 - cranberries
 - apricots

1. Mix all dry ingredients in a bowl (except fruit).

2. Separately mix honey and oil well. Pour over dry ingredients and mix well.

3. Place muesli on a large baking tray.

4. Bake at 150°C (300°F) for 20 minutes or until golden. Stir the mixture half way through so it cooks evenly.

5. Let it cool on the bench and then add sultanas or other dried fruit.

You can add any other fruits and nuts - this recipe is very flexible.

This will store in an airtight container in your pantry for several months.

I use a mixture of finely cut oats and whole oats for a more interesting texture. However you can use either if you do not have both.

Jumbo Rolled Oats

These are oats that have just been rolled and not blended. They are great for muesli (granola) or bars as they give a great texture. It is often good to mix jumbo oats with finer cut oats so you get both texture and fast cooking.

This is a fantastic healthy alternative to dairy cream. It is smooth and has a lot of body.

Whipped Cashew Cream

MAKES 1½ CUPS

1 cup cashew nuts

½ cup water

optional: 2 tablespoons honey or date puree

optional: 1 drop of vanilla essence

1. Put all ingredients into a blender or use a stick blender.

2. Blend well until smooth.

The cream is very nice with just water and cashew nuts, however add the vanilla and honey of you want a sweet version.

To make this amazing add a can of pears (with juice) instead of the water and you have cashew and pear cream.

A classic smoothie that I love and is regularly on our menu at Revive.

Classic Strawberry Smoothie

MAKES 2 X 1 CUP SERVES

1 ripe banana

1 cup soy, almond or rice milk

1 tablespoon honey (or date puree)

1 cup frozen strawberries

1. Put all ingredients into a blender or use a stick blender.

2. Blend well until smooth.

You can use fresh strawberries if they are in season - however add some cubes of ice to help thicken the smoothie and keep it cold.

You can purchase almond milk now in most supermarkets and it is an excellent product - however is very expensive compared to dairy or soy milk. You can make your own very simply and the price works out similar to regular milk when I have done some calculations. Like most good things it just takes a little preparation and planning.

Almond Milk

MAKES 5 CUPS

¾ cup whole raw almonds

4 cups filtered water

8 dates soaked in boiling water for 5 minutes

1 pinch salt

optional: 1 drop vanilla essence

1. Put all ingredients into a blender. A food processor or stick blender may suffice, but will not produce as creamy a milk.

2. Blend for around 2 minutes or until creamy. Use as high a speed as possible. You want creamy milk, not water and small pieces of almonds.

3. You can use straight away or you can store in the fridge for around 5 days. You will have to stir or shake each time you use it as the ingredients will separate.

4. Use as you would normal milk.

If you do not like the brown flecks you can use blanched almonds (the ones without the brown skins) or pour through a strainer or sieve.

You can use cashew or brazil nuts to make different flavoured milks. See which one you like best.

If you are in a hurry you just use 2 tablespoons of honey instead of the dates.

To make almond or nut cream, simply reduce the amount of water.

Dates

Dates are an excellent sweetener that we use extensively at Revive. When diced they are also an excellent alternative to sultanas or raisins. Dates are generally the cheapest of all the dried fruits available so they are economical to use often.

A Revive classic and my favourite smoothie.

Boysenberry Smoothie

MAKES 2 X 1 CUP SERVES

1 ripe banana

1 cup boysenberries

1 tablespoon honey or
date puree

1 cup rice, almond or
soy milk

1. Put all ingredients into a blender or use a stick blender.

2. Blend well until smooth.

3. Serve immediately.

The perfect dessert. I love fruit salads in summer when fruit is so fresh, plentiful and sweet. The key to an excellent fruit salad is using more exotic ingredients and not using basics like banana, oranges and apples.

Tropical Fruit Salad

MAKES 8 X 1 CUP SERVES

250g (9oz) red grapes
(about 1½ cups)

½ orange rock
melon (cantaloupe)

½ green honeydew melon

½ pineapple

¼ medium watermelon

1. Cut the melons in half, scoop out any seeds and cut off the skin.

2. Skin the pineapple and cut out the core. Wash and separate the grapes.

3. Dice all fruit into large 2cm (1in) chunks.

4. Mix all together.

Make sure you do not add sugar or any sweetening to fruit salads - keep it raw and natural!

If you want to prepare ahead of time make sure you put the fruit salad in the fridge with cling wrap.

This is a lovely soothing hot drink or for when you need a pickup. It will also make you feel better when you are feeling down or sick.

Hot Honey, Lemon & Ginger Soother

MAKES 2 X 250ML CUPS

1 sprig of fresh ginger unpeeled (about the size of your thumb)

2 tablespoons honey

juice of 2 lemons

4 lemon slices

boiling water to top of cup or glass

1. Slice ginger into thin strips and put into a glass with lemon juice, lemon slices and honey.

2. Pour boiling water over it and stir.

3. Stand for several minutes to let the flavours mingle.

4. Stir again and serve with the ginger and lemon in the cup/glass.

For added therapeutic benefits, use manuka honey.

Lemons

Lemons are an awesome fruit. The juice adds a sour taste that balances with the other ingredients to achieve an awesome flavour. It is also the perfect addition to drinking water. Make sure you grow a lemon tree or have them in your fruit bowl regularly. You can also grate the rind and add to salads for an extra zing.

This has to be the easiest hot breakfast. Resist the urge to put piles of sugar and cream on it and opt for a healthy version like this one to really set your day up for success. One of my recipe testers for this book gave this recipe to her children. They said "this is the best porridge ever" to which their Mum replied "but it is just porridge". This is evidence of how you can take something old and boring and dress it up with exciting flavours to make it taste great!

Porridge (Oatmeal)

MAKES 1 CUP SERVE

½ cup fine rolled oats (oatmeal)

1 cup cold water

pinch salt

½ cup frozen blueberries

1 tablespoon liquid honey

2 tablespoons sliced almonds

optional: milk of your choice

1. Put the oats, water and salt into a smallish pot on high heat.

2. Keep stirring and when it becomes thick and bubbling, turn the heat down and keep stirring for another 30 seconds.

3. Pour into a bowl and top with the yummy additions.

You can also use whole or jumbo oats, however you will have to cook longer at a lower temperature.

This recipe is very flexible and you can add any combination of nuts, fruit and healthy toppings.

Almonds

An excellent nut that is great in milks, sliced on salads and on breakfasts. It comes in many forms including natural, blanched, slivered, chopped and fine.

A lovely tropical smoothie.

Mango Smoothie

MAKES 2 X 1 CUP SERVES

400g (12oz) can of mango
slices or 1 large
fresh mango

1 cup soy, almond or
rice milk

1 tablespoon honey or
date puree

1 ripe banana

pinch ground nutmeg

1. Put all ingredients into a blender or use a stick blender.

2. Blend until smooth.

3. Serve immediately and garnish with some nutmeg.

An excellent healthy alternative to a chocolate milkshake!

Carob Ice

MAKES 2 X 1 CUP SERVES

2 cups ice cubes

2 tablespoons
carob powder

1 cup milk of your choice

1. Combine ingredients in a blender and process until smooth.

Depending on your blender and ice size you may need to add more milk to keep the blender going.

This is a great way to have a portable breakfast that you can drink on the way to work. It is really quick and you can also fire in some super-foods as well to increase its nutrition!

Muesli Smoothie

MAKES 1 LARGE SERVE (2 CUPS)

1 large ripe banana

1 tablespoon honey

½ cup rolled oats or toasted muesli

1 cup soy, almond or rice milk

optional: ¼ avocado

optional: 6 prunes (dried plums)

optional: 10 Almonds (for protein)

1. Put all ingredients (including any or all optional ingredients) into blender or use a stick blender.

2. Blend until smooth.

3. Garnish with a sprinkle of muesli on top or mix through if you like a textured smoothie.

If you plan to drink this through a straw make sure you blend well and do not add muesli at the end.

Add super foods like flax (linseed) oil and/or bee pollen if you use them.

Avocado adds great healthy fats and gives an amazing smooth texture.

If you have bananas that are getting too ripe, peel them and put them in the freezer. They make great smoothies.

Prunes (Dried Plums)

These add excellent flavour and sweetness to smoothies and have a unique taste.

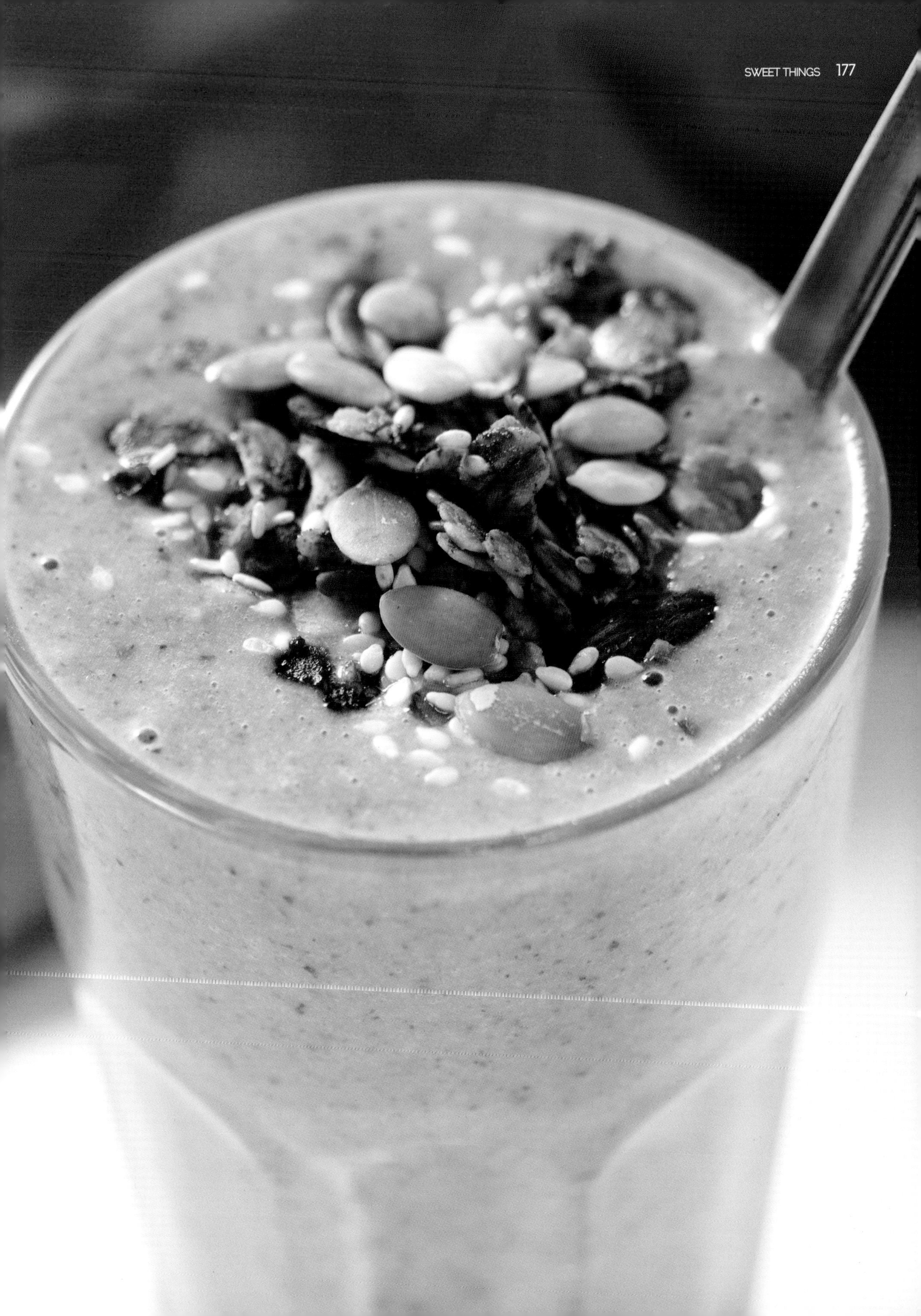

Step-by-Step

Use this step-by-step guide to help you customise your own recipes. Simply follow the instructions to create dishes based on your favourite ingredients and the ingredients you have available at the time.

Please note that you will need a little cooking intelligence to make these work and that the suggested serving sizes are a very rough guide. But give them a go and your cooking skills will quickly improve.

See my first book "The Revive Cafe Cookbook" for step-by-step guides for making a curry, a smoothie, a salad, a stir fry or fritters.

Step-by-Step Soup

Soups are wonderfully warming and very versatile.   Make extra and store in your freezer!

Just keep firing ingredients into the pot and cook until all the ingredients are soft!

ROUGH GUIDE: Will make 12 x 1 cup serves or 3 litres (3qt).

1 Base
put into a large pot and saute for 5 minutes or until soft

2 Flavour
stir in to briefly heat

3 Veges
add to pot - this is the main defining flavour of your soup

---

add all:

2 onions diced

2 carrots diced

2 stalks celery diced

2 tablespoons oil

4 cloves garlic

optional:

2 tablespoons freshly chopped ginger or ginger puree

1 red capsicum (bell pepper) finely chopped

---

choose 1:

2 teaspoons cumin

¼ teaspoon cinnamon

½ teaspoon nutmeg

1 tablespoon Indian curry paste

1 tablespoon Thai curry paste (red, green, yellow)

1 teaspoon onion powder

2 teaspoons mixed herbs

2 teaspoons smoked paprika

---

choose 2: (4 cups total)

pumpkin roughly diced

kumara (sweet potato) roughly diced

frozen corn

potatoes chopped

carrots roughly diced

leeks sliced (add with base)

mushrooms halved (add with base)

870,912
different combinations

4 Protein
add to pot

5 Liquid
add tomatoes/water and simmer for 30-40 minutes - then add the creamy ingredients

6 Final Touches
add to finalise the flavour

choose 1:

2 x 400g (14oz) cans chickpeas (garbanzo beans)

2 x 400g (14oz) cans beans (white, black, red kidney, black-eyed)

1 cup dried red lentils

1 cup dried brown lentils

1 cup split peas

1 cup soup mix (with lentils, split peas, barley)

---

choose 1:

1½ litres (1½ quarts) boiling water

2 x 400g (14oz) cans chopped tomatoes + 1 litre (1 quart) boiling water

add extra 2 cups boiling water here if you have lentils in step 4

optional choose 1:

1 cup almond cream

1 cup cashew cream

1 cup coconut cream

4 tablespoons peanut butter mixed with 1 cup water

---

add:

1 tablespoon salt (possibly more)

2 tablespoons honey or date puree (optional)

choose 1 and add when soup is finished as a garnish: (½ cup)

½ cup chopped coriander (cilantro)

½ cup chopped parsley

½ cup chopped spring onions

7 Blend?
keep as is for a chunky soup or blend with stick blender for smooth

8 Check
for saltiness, sweetness, flavour and texture and adjust if necessary

Step-by-Step Breakfast

Start with a good hearty breakfast and give your body and mind the energy to do amazing things!

Prepare the grains (cold or cooked) and sprinkle all of the remaining ingredients on top.

ROUGH GUIDE: Makes 1 large serving around 2-3 cups.

1 Whole Grains

choose 1: (½ to 1 cup)

rolled oats raw

rolled oats cooked (oatmeal)

quinoa cooked or reheated

rice cooked or reheated

millet cooked

5 grain breakfast cooked or reheated

quinoa or millet flakes

2 Fresh Fruit

choose 3: (1 to 2 cups)

chopped banana

fresh strawberries or blueberries

grated apple

chopped orange

mandarin segments

chopped pear

grapes

sliced mango

chopped nectarine or peach

sliced kiwifruit

3 Other Fruit

choose 1: (¼ to ½ cup)

sultanas or raisins

cranberries

frozen boysenberries

frozen blueberries

chopped dried apricots

chopped dried dates

canned pineapple or peaches

11,404,800
different
combinations

4 Protein > 5 Power Foods > 6 Milk

Protein
choose 1: (1 tablespoon)

slivered or chopped almonds

SLAP (ground sunflower, linseeds, almonds and pumpkin seeds)

sesame seeds sprinkled

tahini (sesame seeds paste)

unsweetened yoghurt

Power Foods
optional choose 1 (or more):

½ teaspoon bee pollen

½ teaspoon maca powder

1 tablespoon flaxseed oil

2 tablespoons goji berries

1 tablespoon chia seeds

Milk
choose 1: (½ cup)

rice milk

almond milk (see page 166)

oat milk

soy milk

Step-by-Step Frittata

Select a round baking dish approximately 25cm (10in) in diameter.
Pre-cook the vegetables and onions and add them to a pan with the extras. Pour over the egg mix.
Bake at 150°C (300°F) for around 20-40 minutes or until just cooked. A bigger dish and shallower pan will reduce time.

Rough guide: this will make around 4-5 serves.

1 Base
fry in a pan

add all:

2 large onions

1 tablespoon oil

2 Egg Mix
add to bowl and mix well with a fork

add:

10 eggs well beaten

1 teaspoon salt

optional:

½ cup cream or milk

1,296
different combinations

3 Veges
in a pan add onion mix with the following

4 Extras
add flavour and then pour over egg mix

5 Garnish
add contrasting colours after cooking is completed

choose 2 (around 4 cups total):

2 cups frozen spinach (defrosted and water squeezed out)

2 cups cooked potatoes

2 cups roasted pumpkin and/or kumara (sweet potato)

2 cups cooked leeks

2 cups frozen corn

2 cups feta cheese

2 cups pan-fried zucchini (courgettes) chopped

2 cups pan-fried mushrooms

1 large red onion diced

choose 1:

1 teaspoon mixed herbs

3 chilli peppers finely chopped

2 cups olives

choose 1:

parsley

red capsicum (bell pepper)

1 cup grated feta or brie cheese

Step-by-Step Dip

Dips are great as a spread for sandwiches, dipping into or as a meal accompaniment.

You can use a food processor (s-blade) for any dip. A blender or stick blender will only work for runnier dips. Simply blend all ingredients until smooth.

Rough guide: this will make around 3-4 cups.

1 Base
add to blender

choose 1:

2 x 400g (14oz) cans chickpeas (garbanzo beans)

2 x 400g (14oz) cans red kidney, black, back-eyed or white beans

2 cups cashew nuts, sunflower seeds or almonds + 1 cup water

400g (14oz) can tomatoes

2 Binding
add to blender

optional add 1:

2 avocados peeled

4 tablespoons oil

2 tablespoons tahini (sesame seed paste)

3 tablespoons peanut butter

3 Flavour
add to blender

choose 1:

4 cups fresh basil

2 cups roasted pumpkin or kumara (sweet potato)

2 cups roasted beetroot

2 red capsicum (bell peppers) raw or roasted

1 cup frozen spinach (defrosted and drained)

1 cup olives

2 roasted eggplant (aubergine)

1 cup sun-dried tomatoes

½ cup roasted garlic

330,750 different combinations

4 Extras
add to blender

5 Season
add to blender

6 Garnish
sprinkle on top

optional choose 1:

½ cup feta cheese

½ cup walnuts

½ cup poppy seeds

¼ teaspoon cayenne pepper

2 chillies

add:

1 teaspoon salt

choose 1:

3 tablespoons lemon juice

3 tablespoons lime juice

2 tablespoons sweet chilli sauce

optional choose 1:

1 cup parsley

1 cup fresh coriander (cilantro)

1 teaspoon curry powder, cumin, coriander or turmeric

optional choose 1:

finely chopped parsley

pinch cayenne pepper

1 teaspoon poppy seeds

1 teaspoon sesame seeds (white or black)

1 teaspoon cumin seeds

7 Check
for saltiness, flavour, sweetness, texture and adjust

Step-by-Step Lasagne

Lasagnes are easiest when you prepare all the sauces and fillings first. Then just layer them up.

3 layers of pasta with 2 layers of fillings. Put tomato sauce in every layer and white sauce in one layer and on top. Use a dish around 20 x 30cm (8 x 12 in). Cook at 180°C (350°F) for around 40-60 minutes or until cooked through.

Rough guide: this will make around 6-8 serves.

1 Pasta
use 3 layers

2 Sauce
for the bottom and top of each layer

3 Veges
bottom layer

---

choose 1:

wholemeal wheat lasagne

tofu sheets

lasagne egg noodles

thin crepes

you can use fresh or dry pasta for this dish

---

choose 1 for layers:

6 cups Italian tomato sauce (page 157)

healthy store-bought tomato or pasta sauce

use for topping:

3 cups white cashew sauce (page 152)

---

choose 3: (5 cups total)

roast pumpkin

roast kumara (sweet potato)

roast capsicum (bell pepper)

frozen spinach

sauteed mushrooms

sauteed onions

sauteed zucchini (courgettes)

broccoli lightly cooked

add ½ teaspoon salt

677,376
different combinations

4 **Protein**
top layer

5 **Flavour**
add with protein

6 **Garnish**
add on top

choose 1:

2 x 400g (14oz) cans chickpeas (garbanzo beans)

1 cup brown or green (puy) lentils cooked with 4 cups water and drained

600g (21oz) tofu sliced or crumbled and sauteed with a little oil

2 x 400g cans beans (red kidney, black, black-eyed, white)

2 cups feta cheese cubed

add ½ teaspoon salt

choose 1:

1 teaspoon dried sage

1 teaspoon ground coriander (cilantro)

¼ teaspoon cayenne pepper

1 teaspoon mixed herbs

1 cup fresh mixed herbs

1 teaspoon smoked paprika

½ teaspoon nutmeg

choose 1 or more:

½ cup freshly chopped parsley

½ cup pumpkin seeds

½ cup poppy seeds

1 cup olives sliced

Recipe Index